# HAVING IT ALL

# *Erica Kane*

♥♥♥♥♥♥♥♥♥♥♥♥♥♥♥♥♥♥♥♥♥♥♥♥♥♥♥♥♥♥

# HAVING IT
# *A*LL

♥♥♥♥♥♥♥♥♥♥♥♥♥♥♥♥♥♥♥♥♥♥♥♥♥♥♥♥♥♥

abc
**daytime
press**

**HYPERION**

NEW YORK

*Watch Erica Kane every weekday on All My Children.*

Erica Kane is a fictional character from ABC's  *All My Children.*

**Library of Congress Cataloging-in-Publication Data**

Having it all / by Erica Kane.—1st ed.
  p.  cm.
 ISBN 0–7868-6363-3
  1. All my children (Television program)  2. Kane, Erica (Fictitious character)
3. Conduct of life.  4. Success.
PN1992.77.A5H38   1997                                    97—3152
791.45'72—dc21                                            CIP

Designed by *Nicholas A. Bernini*

FIRST EDITION

10  9  8  7  6  5  4  3  2  1

# Dedication

Bags of mail pour into my office every week from people like you, women and men whose lives I have touched; some, even transformed. Many of you ask the same question: "How do you **do** it, Erica? How do you manage to Have It ALL? And can I Have It ALL, too?"

For your sake, I hope so. But can I, Erica Kane, guarantee you the same glory and success I have achieved? Sorry. C'est **impossible**. I can but share my wisdom, my lessons hard-learned.

This book is an outpouring straight from the heart, a love letter to you, my adoring and adored legion of loyal fans. May it serve as a silver lining in the cloud of life.

I remain humbly and gratefully yours,

Erica Kane

# Acknowledgments

There is no way I could have written this elegant, slim, breezy—yet erudite—volume without my Creator. Nor could I have done it all by myself without inspiration from other writers too numerous to mention. I'm good, but nobody's *that* good!

To all my friends in the Pine Valley Writer Support Group I blow a big kiss! You know who you are—past, present, and future. Thank you!

My editor, MCS—who was always supportive and sometimes right—helped me, too. Kiss-kiss!

# 1

## Self-Love

*I*'m reclined in an Adirondack chair under a willow tree in the garden of my six-acre estate, Linden House. I write these words on the vellum pages of a silk-bound notebook with my initials emblazoned on the cover in scarlet thread. This is my third book, dear readers, my first without a coauthor.

Though I confess to being a trifle nervous, the birds are trilling their encouragement, the sun is beaming her warm confidence, and so—I begin!

Because I'm a naturally generous, outgoing person with successes and accomplishments far beyond the norm, people constantly try to pick my brains. Fans stand in awe. My beauty, success, and serenity make jaws the world over drop. They—like you—beg to know how I did it. They implore me in person, write letters, send e-mail.

ERICA KANE

If I tried to answer each and every one personally, there'd be no time to eat or sleep. That's why I'm writing this book. How could I *not* hold the torch aloft to light your way?

The biggest secret to Having It ALL is understanding it's simply a state of mind. Therefore, anyone can achieve it. Easily. Though not necessarily at the level I enjoy.

The first step is to love yourself. Totally and without reservation. You're perfect, just the way you are!

Oscar Wilde, the aptly named and justly famous playwright, said, "To love oneself is the beginning of a lifelong romance." *That* is genius. My personal love affair with myself has been the most satisfying relationship I've ever had, and I'm not ashamed to admit it. I think I'm the most glorious human being ever born.

Love is the most important thing there is. It's my reason for living, the motivation for everything I do.

All love begins with self-love, psychiatrists say, and on that score, at least, I believe them. It makes sense! How can you love someone else if you don't love yourself? Much less Have It ALL?

But be ever vigilant. You mustn't confuse self-love with selfishness. Often it's hard to tell the difference, but they are *not* the same. Self-love is fun! It's being the best you can be, for the right reasons. It's not about vanity or egotism.

Even as a child, I was often falsely accused of selfishness. Jealousy was behind those sandbox attacks, of course, but that's another story (covered fully in my first best-seller, *Raising Kane*, chapters one through five). Self-love is about

4

(1983; credit: BOB SACHA/ABC)

Even Michelangelo pales compared to me.

honoring the unique wonderfulness of your own heart and soul.

Here's an exercise. Take a hand mirror to a corner of your home where you feel especially comfortable. Look deeply into your own eyes and express out loud how much you love yourself. Maybe you're a hard worker, a loving parent, a dedicated rocket scientist. Say so! Give voice to your most lovable qualities out loud while gazing into your own eyes. If your voice has a grating quality, smooth it out. Mimic the mellifluous tone of someone else—like me. Or my friend Jackson Montgomery. It's okay to laugh. The important thing is to *mean the words.*

Loving yourself is the first step on the road to Having It ALL. Trust yourself. You couldn't have gotten this far without superb instincts, could you? You wouldn't have had the sense and discernment to come to me for help.

Many of our mothers raised us to love others, love God, our country, our families. Admirable sentiments indeed. Yet they omitted the most vital element—self, self, self! Even my own mother, who was a saint, neglected to encourage self-love. Perhaps she thought I'd pick it up by osmosis. Whether Waterford or those little cartoon-adorned jelly glasses, or—like myself, Lalique—we are all vessels waiting to be filled. Children hunger for knowledge. As you guide yours, think of me.

One of the most thrilling benefits of self-love is you're never lonely. How can boredom exist when there's always that delightful someone (yourself) to lavish attention on, to love! My own company is equally as fascinating as friends like the New Orleans Saints or captains of industry Warren Buffett and Tom Murphy. When you honestly love yourself, curling up with a good book—such as this one—at home is just as satisfying as an elegant dinner at Nexus in New York City.

Another benefit of self-love is robust health. We naturally take care of what we love. That means eating right, exercising, getting plenty of sleep, having regular checkups with doctors and dentists. Spa visits are a must and the three *M*'s are mandatory: *M*assage, *M*anicure, and *M*oisturize. Our bodies are our temples. Frequent worship is required.

You can always tell when a person stops loving him or herself. They let themselves go. They fail to apply sunscreen. Their faces soon appear to have been carved from apples. Muscle tone goes from buffed to blubber. They yawn a lot. They lose their hair and their friends. Falling out of love with yourself can have dire health consequences, which is why self-love must always be nourished!

Treat yourself! . . . Buy the freshest fruits and vegetables available. Be adventurous. Don't judge a fruit by its repellent appearance. Often the most disgusting skin covers the sweetest flesh. Eat them slowly, savoring every luscious bite. Drink at least eight glasses of clean fresh water every day. Lower the amount of fat in your diet!

There is no better exercise on earth than a brisk walk. For those of us cursed with celebrity, fleeing the paparazzi is a daily aerobic workout. For the rest of you, Mother Earth is a beautiful thing to observe, whether your path is through city or country. Each season, each time of day holds new wonders. You can listen to music while you walk. Breathe deeply. Swing your arms. Appreciate everything!

If you want it ALL, there's no room in your head for anything but positive thinking. Avoid negative thinking like the plague! It's very bad for your skin.

Those of us who love ourselves have no time for negative thoughts. We're too busy taking care of ourselves, eating right, taking brisk walks, jetting off to the Caribbean on volcano hunts if we feel adventurous, or to Biarritz to bask in the sun if we need pampering.

You mustn't think those of us who already Have It ALL don't slip into old patterns of misbehavior and make mistakes. I personally have made several. You have to be a risktaker to Have It ALL, and nobody wins every battle. The trick is to learn from mistakes, move on.

The easiest way to learn from mistakes is to remember that everything happens for a reason, and always turns out the way it's supposed to. That's just how life is. When you're knocked down, there's no point lying there, crying and moaning. You stand up tall, admit your mistake, and start all over again. I present the ultimate example in my Phoenix rising from the ashes saga, *Erica Kane: Beyond the Pain*.

Yes, life is what *you* make it. When you love yourself, everything about you is precious. The world opens its arms. Your fondest dreams are guaranteed to come true.

All my life I've been inspired to help others. I was a Brownie scout, a candy striper, and a cheerleader. I taught

(1970s; credit: ABC).

My high school yearbook picture. I love how fresh and wholesome I look. Innocence shines in my eyes.

Vacation Bible School for two weeks. Even as a teenager, it was clear to me how special I was.

Blessed with more gifts and abilities than other young women in my town, I longed to share what I had. My very first job was sales clerk at a fashion boutique in Pine Valley. I was only sixteen, but already my sense of style and design was fine-tuned. Women five times my age trusted my judgment. Why wouldn't they? They had only to look at me to realize I had something they didn't.

Star quality is as good a term as any for the sparkle I radiated wherever I went. I was born to turn heads. Sad to say, when you're lucky enough to be born beautiful, you can easily inspire the worst in others. I'm talking about envy. It's unfair, but the small-minded among us will always resent you.

It's best to let jealous, unfounded criticism roll off your back. If you want to Have It ALL, you must fight the all-too-human urge to sit in judgment of others. Judge Not Lest Ye Be Judged is my credo.

Never forget that whatever you project in life is what you get back. Thus when you love yourself enough, the rest of the world can't help but jump on the bandwagon. Adoration is contagious!

It's your job to set goals. It isn't enough to want to be rich, famous, thin, and beautiful. Formulate a plan! Lawyers, accountants, and bankers are good at plans, but as I'm sure you've noticed, few of them Have It ALL. You, on the other hand, see goal-setting as an artist sees a clean canvas. Paint your hopes and dreams. They can come true!

Never be afraid to seek advice. If everyone who ever came

to my rescue over the years linked arms, the line would stretch to Timbuktu. People love to help. Take advantage of it. And don't forget to offer a heartfelt thank you.

Because I'm nonjudgmental, open to suggestion, and as eager to learn as I am to teach, my road to success has been shorter than most. When it comes to the work ethic, nobody puts her flawlessly powdered nose to the grindstone with more devotion and determination than I do.

Why? Because hard work pays off. I'd never be where I am today if I hadn't dedicated myself heart and soul to honest labor. I'm not afraid to get my hands dirty.

My mother loved to quote her mother's favorite saying: "When love and skill work together, expect a masterpiece." She was right. You get out of a project what you put into it.

In other words, dear readers, Having It ALL requires your best effort. In everything. Always. Luckily, this comes naturally to me. I strive for excellence the same way I breathe. Who needs to think? Just do it!

I know I make it sound easy. In a most profound way, it *is*. But so is dancing *Swan Lake* or surfing in Hawaii—*if* you know how. The goal is to soar above the stage or the ocean without effort, only with grace. Every bird learns to fly. When you love yourself, every flight becomes an art form.

Jeremy Hunter, the famous artist and former Buddhist monk, taught me that. Jeremy also accused me of never having an unexpressed thought. He didn't intend it as a compliment, but, ha ha, of course, it was!

Rarely did a day go by without Jeremy spouting one of his favorite catch phrases: "Be the water, not the rock." We must

This is a lovely portrait of me and the artist Jeremy Hunter.

move past obstacles. One of the best benefits of self-love is you don't carry around a lot of unspoken misery. Get rid of it! Go with the flow. If something occurs to you, say it! Don't hold it inside where it festers. Give it light. Call it by its right name. That way, fear can never control you.

Come to think of it, Alcoholics Anonymous, grandparent of all the marvelous Twelve-Step programs, teaches members to cultivate an "attitude of gratitude." The rewards of having such an attitude are enormous.

If I were to tell you everything I'm grateful for in my life, this book would never end. While others brood, I count my millions of blessings. After all, I love myself, and why not? I Have It ALL.

# 2

## Pitfalls

So far I have instructed you in the most important requirement for Having It ALL: self-love. Believe me, we only scratched the surface. I put the ball in your hands. It's up to you to run with it.

Wait! Not so fast! First we have to discuss the pitfalls. There are many.

But don't be discouraged. Nothing worth having comes easy. And while pitfalls can slow you down or even sideline you on the fast track to glory, they can—later—make for marvelous dinner conversation and even scintillating reading. Still, they're best avoided, so study your map. Consult it often. Identify the hairpin turns, the speed bumps, all the danger points on the road. Know your enemy. When you meet an obstacle, consider it a challenge.

The major challenge I've faced on the road to Having It

ALL is my tendency to trust the wrong people. My own integrity leads me to imagine honor in others. This character flaw sabotaged me all my life, until finally I learned to trust myself first. Whatever your character flaws are, don't let them rule you.

And don't dwell on the past! The pitfalls I stumbled into are history, but you should be warned. Sometimes one leads to another. Often, I not only trusted the wrong people, I blamed them for making me stumble. Then I fell off a scaffold, injured my back, became addicted to painkillers. Recovery taught me to accept responsibility for my own mistakes, even to forgive the treacherous weasels who betrayed my trust.

It's hardly news that there are people in this world who feed on generous, good-hearted souls like myself. Evil has many faces. Damon Lazarre, Jonathan Kinder, Billy Clyde Tuggle, and Lars Bogard spring immediately to mind. Also Goldie Kane, Connie Wilkes, Joanna Yeager, and Helga Voynitzeva. There are others, whose actions were more recent and every bit as heinous, but legal considerations prevent me from printing their names. No matter how often these types of vile worthless creatures slither into your life, remember: In the end, nobody can take advantage of you unless you let them.

I suppose—since nothing is impossible—another con man could stroll into my life and attempt to take advantage of me. Let him try. By now, you see, having learned from my past, I refuse to repeat it—the bad parts, that is. I know what to look for. If anyone's eyeing me with malevolent intent, I'll spot him. Or her. In a heartbeat.

Beware those of the drooling scowl and scuttling crablike gait. I cross the street to avoid anyone with the teensiest hint of envy, the smallest bent toward brooding. Also liars. I never waste time with people who can't tell the simple truth! Lying is one of the most unhealthy things you can do. It's soul-crunching even to be around people who lie.

Stay away from drugs. Painkillers were my personal downfall, but every drug has the potential to harm. Aspirin, laxatives, vitamins, even penicillin can be abused, so treat them carefully! Make sure you know everything there is to know about any drug you take. Including alcohol, which we all know is a drug.

I never had a problem with alcohol. French Champagne was the only apéritif I really liked, and a few sips was always more than enough. After dinner, I occasionally enjoyed a small brandy. But I liked painkillers so much I lied, cheated, and stole to get them, so alcohol is too dangerous a drug for me now, thank you. I prefer sparkling water, anyway. I recommend it highly.

Unscrupulous pushers tout drugs as harmless, recreational. Don't buy into such nonsense. There is no such thing as harmless or recreational drugs. Any use can lead to abuse, and the result of such abuse, according to Narcotics Anonymous, can be only one of three things: jails, institutions, or death. There is nothing glamorous about drugs. As my beloved brother Mark could tell you. Poor Mark succumbed to the dark underside of show business. While gaining success as a songwriter specializing in the upbeat, he foolishly became caught in the sticky web of cocaine addiction. He lied, cheated, and stole—even from me—to support his foul habit.

Some addicts wake up to the damage they are doing to themselves and their families only after the close call of a family member. Mark's step-grandchild Bonnie could have died a horrible death had she eaten any of those "play cookies" she made with the "funny flour" she found hidden by Mark. And I received quite a jolt when my beloved Bianca nearly took one of my "vitamin" pills.

Although many would hold the drug pushers fully responsible, Mark and I had to face our own culpability. We were no better than the lowest denizens of Front Street.

Oh. I probably should have mentioned hate as the first pitfall. . . . Hate, in any of its ugly forms, is something you must avoid at all cost! Hate is not a family value.

Hate can also kill. As a matter of fact, hate *does* kill. The good news is it's a lot easier to recognize hate than untrustworthiness. I don't have to tell you what hate is. Tragically, we see it everywhere. We're often offended by it on a daily basis. Hate is the *opposite* of love, and we want no part of it!

So, if there is hate gnawing away at your life, get rid of it! How? Speak out! However the repulsive emotion manifests itself, call it that! To the speaker's face! If it's bigotry, racism, sexism, sadism, whatever, say so! Then leave—quickly and gracefully. Don't dally with haters, for heaven's sake. Why subject yourself to their poison?

(1996; credit: ANN LIMONGELLO/ABC)

At the place where my life changed forever—The Betty Ford Center.

Once in a blue moon, a hater can be transformed. I've seen it happen. But you cannot depend on miracles. You are not responsible for their metamorphosis. Your job is you! So root the malicious troublemakers out of your life without mercy. Cut them off! When you love yourself and want it all, there is no room for anyone's hate on your plate.

As a general rule, steer clear of fanatics. This is a pitfall I've experienced many times. For who-knows-what cosmic purpose, wild-eyed maniacs are drawn to me on a regular basis. My close friend Janet Green once observed that a certain fanatic we both knew and loved "used up all the oxygen in the room." Obviously, associating with this type of person is not good for your health. Try to limit the number of fanatics in your circle of friends. One or two is plenty.

Fatigue is also a no-no. Lack of proper sleep causes unsightly bloating of the eyes and face as well as bad moods. You have only to observe an infant or a small child to realize sleepiness makes us cranky. Figure out how much sleep you need, and make sure you get it.

Never burn your candle at both ends. Treat your natural energy levels with the respect they deserve. When your body tells you to rest, take heed!

I can't underscore enough how crucial it is to listen when your body speaks. Rely on your own instincts above anyone else's, no matter what. If I had done more of that in the past, my life today would be different. Instead, I often ignored my gut feelings, went with others', usually men's. It was painful, but I learned important lessons each time.

It all started with my father, of course.

I know it's fashionably Freudian to blame mothers for every neurosis and crime, but it's not an accident that these theories were dreamed up by men. In my home, for instance, Daddy was the villain. He left us. He walked out on my mother and me, went to Hollywood. (See *Raising Kane* chapters one through ten, eighteen, and twenty-three through twenty-six.)

Little girls abandoned by their daddies almost always have disastrous relationships with men when they grow up. I was no exception. (See the balance of *Raising Kane*.)

My disasters have been splashed on the front pages of newspapers for decades. Most of what they write about me is libelous fabrication, but an occasional honest writer/journalist does cross my path. Their names escape me at present. Oh! Russell Baker has never written an unkind word about me. If you're reading, Russell, thank you!

I'm very nonjudgmental about the media. I've been in their shoes. On the whole, reporters are sincerely after the truth, the whole truth, and nothing but the truth. As a writer myself, I have pity for the press. Like Hamlet, they traffic in the slings and arrows of outrageous fortune.

In spite of the unflattering photographs, unjust rumors, and humiliating lies constantly printed about me, I'm as devoted to the First Amendment of the United States Constitution as Brooke English, maybe even more so. Freedom of the press is number one in my book, as well as in the Bill of Rights. When you Have It ALL, loss of privacy is a major pitfall.

But you needn't avoid the media or treat them like dirt. Simply exercise extreme caution as you would playing polo in a mine field. Every profession employs bad eggs; journalism, unfortunately, also hires snakes and vultures. Nonetheless, the media can't hurt you if you remember two things. Smile. And always tell the truth.

The law is another profession to be wary of. The last thing you need is to appear before a judge. People who Have It ALL stay away from the court system, especially the criminal court system. If you're a magnet for extremists, as I am, you'll need to keep excellent legal counsel on retainer at all times.

I cringe to think where I'd be if I hadn't hired some of the

With my favorite legal counsel, Jackson Montgomery.

finest lawyers in this country. They remain my friends to this day. Paul Martin, Lincoln Tyler, Jackson Montgomery, Trevor Dillon are all valued friends of long standing. However, I never forget that they're lawyers. Except for Trevor, they each spent three years in law school, learning to speak out of both sides of their mouths. Remember that in any dealings you're forced to have with a lawyer.

It's not my intention to bash anyone's profession! My goodness, I made a spectacular living as a model for a long time, and everyone knows modeling is one of the most maligned occupations on earth.

Those lights are hot. It's hard work.

There's more to making it big in the fashion world than perfect features and an ideal figure. Without the sparkle I spoke of earlier, the willingness to smile, be nice to everyone you meet, you're bound to fail.

Anyone who's ever made a joke about models should follow one around all day. The work never ends! Plus you have to carry a heavy bag. It's glamorous, all right, but hardly the piece of cake many imagine. But I digress.

*Depression* is a pitfall that can lay low even the mighty. It's a dismal condition that turns delightful people into bores and malcontents. Never let it get a foothold in your life!

My dear friend Tad Martin, my cohost of "The Cutting Edge," a television show I created, told me the best cure for depression was to stop thinking about yourself and do something kind for someone else. To cheer up a loved one, Tad once wore a feathered chicken suit to a formal dinner party. I wouldn't go that far, and neither should you, but why not

Here I am modeling casualwear in my early career.

send a card to a shut-in, or take your old magazines to a nursing home? It can't hurt.

Another surefire depression-lifter is a smile. That's all. You don't even have to have anything to smile about, just use the muscles, make yourself grin. Scientists have proved the simple act of smiling releases endorphins or whatever into your system, which creates a feeling of well-being. It's true! Try it. (Fear of wrinkles must be dispelled. See the three *M*'s page 7)

Depression has reared its ugly head more than once in my presence. When my mother died, for instance, I was inconsolable for quite a while. Pure self-indulgence, of course, but it took its toll. Finally, I remembered Tad's advice, wrote a big fat check to the American Cancer Society, and presto, my depression lifted. Simply reaching out, sharing my good fortune brought back the sunshine. Thank you, Tad!

I don't want to make short shrift of grief. When someone you love dies, grief is inevitable. It's a necessary process with five famous stages of which depression is only one. I wouldn't wish it on my worst enemy. It's when the depression stage of grief goes on for too long that it becomes a pitfall. Balance is the trick. Everything in moderation is okay. Never deny yourself permission to feel!

Guilt! Again, reams of paper could be consumed on the subject of guilt. More precious energy is squandered on guilt than on sit-ups. Unless you intentionally set out to harm yourself or others, which of course neither of us would ever do, we have no reason to feel guilty!

Women are particularly susceptible to the loathsome burden of guilt. Unless we're the parent of an underage child, it's not our job to take responsibility for others! I beg you to free yourselves from this negative emotion.

Guilt sours the recipe for a happy disposition faster than vinegar in a chocolate soufflé. What a waste! Other than dragging you down, it serves no purpose. Like giving others the upper hand in your life, guilt can happen only if you let it!

Since loving yourself means taking responsibility for everything you say and do, there's never any need for guilt. In fact, I sincerely suggest you remove it from your vocabulary entirely, as I have.

A common pitfall in *my* experience, but rare for the rest of the population, I hope, is believing someone is dead when they're really alive and well. Never accept that a person is gone unless you have evidence, i.e., physical proof. If you lack proof, you'll be wise to stay vigilantly alert to any possibility. I can't tell you the number of times I was taken by surprise. Practically everyone I know has been presumed dead at least once. I myself started a scrapbook of my own faux obituaries.

There's nothing quite like the stun of discovery when what seems like a ghost is in truth a living person you thought was dead. There's nothing you can do to prepare for it. If you're married to the person, it's even more bizarre. If you're reading this in West Virginia you might call Dixie Cooney Martin; she'll tell you—the main thing is to remain calm.

Amnesia is another bolt-out-of-the-blue pitfall for which there's no way to prepare. At times, the condition seems almost epidemic. Joe Martin, Chief of Staff of Pine Valley Hospital and a cherished friend, should assign a medical research team to investigate.

Losing your memory is a hideous experience. Suddenly, you're cast adrift. With no past to anchor you, the present and future loom frightening. It's a terrible illness to suffer. The only way I can think of to protect yourself is to avoid head injuries, or traumas of any sort, including emotional ones which can trigger amnesia instantaneously. Be very, very cautious, especially if you visit Pine Valley.

Any sudden onset of mental illness is terrifying. I've been hospitalized several times, and so have some of my friends. There's nothing shameful about a nervous breakdown. The stigma is gradually disappearing, thank goodness. Recovery is always possible because miracles happen every day. Modern science works wonders!

Excessive pride can detour your goals. There's nothing wrong with being proud of yourself, but patting yourself on the back to extreme can be as dangerous a stretching piano wire across your own path. Pride will trip you up every time.

Pitfalls are everywhere. Be fleet of foot, bob and weave. Learn to anticipate and prepare. Above all, never cave in. Never—ever—give up!

# 3

## Money

*W*hew! We've covered how to love your-self and how to steer clear of pitfalls on the road to Having It ALL. Now we get down to specifics.

Money.

Frankly, Having It ALL financially is *everything* it's cracked up to be and more. I've made, lost, and remade several fortunes so far, and I see no reason why, when the millennium rolls around, I shouldn't be one of the wealthiest people on the planet.

The Bible tells us the love of money is the root of all evil. We're also warned that it's easier for a camel to pass through the eye of a needle than for a rich man to get into heaven. Scary, isn't it? That's why, when I wake up every morning, I thank my Higher Power for making me a woman.

Getting rich is child's play compared to raising a child. Believe me. I've done both.

Money can buy just about everything but love. The right amount in the palm of your hand assures excellent service wherever you go. And why shouldn't it? Money, after all, is the value stick by which we measure a person's worth in this world, and, let's face it, the more you're worth, the better you're treated.

Not that that's the way it *ought* to be. But reality is reality.

Amassing an impressive net worth requires all the skills we've already mentioned, plus a few specialized and sharply honed instincts. Cream always rises to the top.

Think big. Nothing is beyond your reach. There's no limit to the financial security you can enjoy once you set your mind to it. A person who Has It ALL is free from worry about the rent, the phone bill, the astronomical cost of a college education.

Perhaps you're stuck in a job you don't like. Quit! Find a new job. Figure out what you do best, and send out your résumé. Call old family friends, classmates—anyone in your debt. Leave no stone unturned until you're earning a paycheck in your chosen field. Work hard, and learn all you can. Since you love yourself, this is second nature, pure joy. Joy in the workplace always leads to full coffers.

Or you could make money the old-fashioned way. Marry it. A rich, well-loved husband or wife is no slight advantage. They say it's as easy to fall in love with a rich person as a poor one, and my experience certainly bears it out.

Some lucky individuals inherit pots of money, vast estates, international conglomerates. My last husband, Dimitri Marick, falls into this category. He was born with a silver spoon in his mouth, but he'd never declare he Has It ALL. He doesn't.

Getting your money handed to you on a platter is hardly a recipe for happiness. Ask Nina Cortlandt, the daughter of my dear friend Palmer. The rich *are* different. And not always in a good way. In other words, you can be King Midas and still not Have It ALL.

Those of us who rise to the top from nowhere do so unfettered by tiresome family traditions carved in stone. We spout no silly mottoes of honor won or lost, sport no gruesome coats-of-arms. Rather, we burst on the scene with new ideas, fresh solutions! We bring with us the exciting mystique that surrounds a self-made man or woman, a bold robber-baron audacity that adds to our allure. We're born leaders, tough as Marines.

In the long run, it's better to earn money than marry or inherit it. I've had it both ways. Gain a fortune by the glow of your unfurrowed brow and you're far less likely to fritter away your profits.

Once your war chest is full, invest wisely. Always sock away as much as you can afford. At least 10 percent of your paycheck should go promptly into investment growth vehicles, preferably more. Fifty percent isn't too much. The faster you save, the faster you reach your goal.

Thoroughly research and find the best broker or money

manager in your area. Consider his or her advice, then make your own decisions.

Keep in mind bonds are for income, stocks are for growth. Build a portfolio that covers all bases. Transportation, utilities, technology, etc., are among those you can choose from. They call this kind of portfolio "diversified," but it's not complicated. Simply buy stock in companies whose products or services you believe in. Choose bonds the same way. You can't go wrong!

You have to spend money to make money, so listen to your instincts. If, while pondering choices, your Higher Power tells you to buy one hundred shares of Enchantment Cosmetics Common Stock, do so! Loving yourself means getting the highest possible return on your investments.

My mother, bless her heart, was somewhat old-fashioned. She believed even to utter the word *money* out loud was vulgar. "Well-brought-up young ladies don't discuss money," she used to say when I'd ask, for instance, how much was in her savings account. She claimed it was none of my business. I had to teach myself to balance a checkbook.

My mother, like many women of her generation, was horribly conflicted on the subject of money. Almost as conflicted as she was about sex. But that's another chapter.

Yesterday's women saw finances as an unfeminine interest, and shied away from it. What a mistake! They couldn't help transferring that attitude to their daughters, but we can fight it. We have to fight it! With all our strength!

Money is power. It represents the fruit of our labor almost as much as our children. Treat your net worth with respect. Don't be ashamed to be rich. Remember, whatever you have, you earned!

Like most gifts, wealth is a curse and a blessing. The temptation to turn control of your purse strings over to another, usually a lover or spouse, is enormous, but must be resisted! We already agreed money is power, and everyone knows power corrupts. Would you knowingly corrupt someone you love? Of course not! Nor would someone who loves you want to be corrupted. You earned it. It's your responsibility to take care of it.

What could be simpler than that?

Now that you've earned your money, invested it wisely, watched it grow, how do you handle the surplus that pours in? Jump start the global economy!

The world is full of bargains. Go to Paris, Milan, New York, and Los Angeles for designer fashions; Cartagena, Colombia, for emeralds; Istanbul, Turkey, for rugs; and Scotland for cashmere. Insist on quality. Whatever it costs, you're proud to pay for the best.

Be generous. Shower your loved ones with tokens of esteem. Candy Spelling, for example, has two "wrapping rooms" in her mansion where she lovingly wraps presents for family and friends. She Has It ALL!

(Incidentally, the secret to the perfectly presented gift is to wrap the top and bottom of the box separately. This way, the recipient need only untie the ribbon and open the box to find your offering. And there are no unsightly balls of torn paper to throw away.)

Never insult someone you love by using your wealth to support him or her. Every adult citizen of the world has the right to be independent! Honor their rights as you expect yours to be honored.

In a restaurant, tip 20 percent, more if the service is extraordinary. You can compute this in your head without pain. Take 10 percent and double it. How hard is that?

Waiting on tables is rough work at low wages. I know. I've been there. A stingy tipper will never make it through the eye of that biblical needle, but those of us who love ourselves know it's better to give than receive.

Give your employees a raise or a bonus every time your ship comes in. Share the wealth! They'll love you for it, and love is more important than money, remember.

Choosing the right charity to support is as easy as choosing the right investments. Whatever group fights for a cause you believe in, write them checks. Big checks. But don't attach strings. Charitable contributions are gifts, and gifts don't have strings.

Over the years I have supported many causes, including the American Cancer Society, AIDS research, homeless shelters, environmental activists, etc., etc. There isn't room to list them all. Some battles are won, some are lost, but investing in what you believe in is always money well spent.

Insist on golden parachute clauses in your contracts, no matter how unpopular it makes you. When money's

(1991; credit: ANN LIMONGELLO/ABC)

My close friends, financiers Warren Buffet and Tom Murphy, advise me on investments.

involved, you have to play hardball. Remember: with a bit of planning, failure in a company can be far more lucrative than success!

Don't gamble. A racehorse is a beautiful animal, but one wrong step, and it's off to the glue factory. The wrong bet can cost you dearly. This does *not* mean that you should not

39

revel in the delights of the Kentucky Derby or Ascot. Give yourself to the gracious social rituals, but keep your hard-earned cash in the bank.

Las Vegas isn't nicknamed "Lost Wages" for nothing. When P. T. Barnum of circus fame said, "There's a sucker born every minute," his time estimate was conservative. The best way to avoid getting hooked on gambling is the same as the best way to avoid drugs. Never start!

I won't forget Benny Sago's sad bout with gambling fever. He was young, blue-collar, and wanted it all—the easy way. By the time he admitted his problem, he had a shoebox full of lottery tickets hidden under his couch. It was pathetic.

Get-rich-quick schemes like lotteries, sweepstakes, chain letters, raffles, etc., are usually con games run by bilkers. Don't fall into their traps! If it sounds too good to be true, it probably is!

If you're blackmailed, refuse to pay. This is a lesson I've had to learn many times. Occasionally, even my closest relatives have tried to blackmail me, but extortion, demanded or given in to, never pays. Stand your ground! Nobody can blackmail you unless you let them.

The truth is, no matter how well stocked your coffers are, some evil wind of fate can blow through and leave you penniless. It's happened to me. Several times. I mean, there I am, on top of the world, riding high, and *whoosh!* The rug's pulled out from under me.

These things happen. It's depressing, but markets crash, businesses fail, husbands keel over and die deeply in debt and lacking insurance. You can be wiped out in a New York minute, left breathless, staring at your empty bankbook.

The solution to that unspeakable possibility is simple and, by now, I hope, familiar. After you survey the damage, learn from whatever mistake you made; sip some aromatic herbal tea, take a deep breath, and start all over again. Love isn't the only thing that's better the second time around. Or the third, fourth, fifth, etc., etc. Every fortune I make, I enjoy more.

Powerful and alluring as money is, there's a reason they call it "filthy lucre." I shudder to think of all the nasty wallets, hands, billfolds, and pockets the average dollar bill passes through before it gets to me. Not to mention the shoddy and unsavory services it pays for.

Turn your nose up at cash. Checks, credit cards, and, best of all, "Bill me" should describe your everyday contact with money. If you collect gold pieces, I'd sterilize them before I played with them if I were you. While it's perfectly fine to talk about money, try not to touch it!

How *much* money you need to Have It ALL is a question of personal preference. One person's castle in Spain is another's shanty by the sea. What counts is collecting enough to give yourself all the rewards you deserve for being as wonderful as you are.

My own needs are modest compared to friends like Donald Trump. A healthy investment portfolio bursting with tax-free municipal bonds, an unrivaled collection of jewelry, real estate, antiques, art, and a bottomless checkbook are all

I require. You might need more. If you do, it's out there. All you have to do is go get it!

Money isn't mysterious. It's the fuel that propels our economy, the means by which we pay our own way. Thanks to one of the greatest inventions of modern times, the pocket calculator, anyone can manage his or her finances. There's nothing to fear! You don't have to be a genius in math to get rich.

Beware of the Internal Revenue Service! They mean business. I strongly urge you to hire a top-notch professional accountant to advise you on taxes. Good luck trying to figure out on your own what the IRS is talking about! They convolute it on purpose, I'm convinced. Never mind! Just pay what you owe and pay it proudly!

This is the greatest country in the world, and if it costs you 38 percent of your income to live here, so what? It's a privilege to be an American. Anyone who doesn't believe that can just go to another country and try to Have It ALL. Good luck.

Every so often a politician lands on the scene with ideas and agendas that mirror my own. You can be sure when Election Day looms in November that candidate's name appears in my checkbook. Support political candidates you believe in, but again: no strings. Don't expect a night in the Lincoln bedroom or chicken fried steak with Bill and Hillary.

I'm a 100 percent red, white, and blue American who puts her money where her mouth is. Unfortunately, my candidates often lose, but who cares? It's the principle that counts.

Let your money work for you instead of against you. Grab your share, but be careful. Don't let the pursuit of wealth get in the way of your main pursuit: happiness. Money can be our hardworking friend, our comfort in old age, but it is *no substitute for love!*

# 4

## *Morality*

*N*ow that you've learned to love yourself, protect yourself from pitfalls, and earn and take care of major chunks of money, it's time to discuss morality.

The Ten Commandments is a good place to begin.

Obey them!

Turn a cold shoulder to false gods. Don't curse. Use colorful regional language instead. My dear friend Opal has honed folksy expletives to a fine art. Go to church (or temple, mosque, oak grove, whatever) once a week for meaningful conversation with your Higher Power on your day of rest. Honor your parents. Do not kill, commit adultery, or steal even a towel from a motel. No lying. No envy. And don't forget the Golden Rule. Love your neighbor as much as you love yourself.

What could be plainer?

But the schism between *understanding* how to live and actually *living* is deep and wide. I've failed in the leap myself. Not counting the false gods and graven images Commandment, I've broken every one. (Unless you consider drugs to be false gods and graven images, in which case, I'm batting 1.000.) I hate to admit it, but—like you—I too am imperfect—to a degree.

And how I've paid for it! Every single time I strayed from the moral path outlined above, I was cut down. Mowed down is more like it. On my knees, pride shattered, hopes dashed. It never fails.

Life is complicated. Moral decisions are forced on us daily. Good and bad, right and wrong, someone's always making us choose. It's exhausting.

Recognizing the difference between right and wrong can wear you out. Sometimes what is wicked can look maddeningly attractive. Watch out! Why? Say it with me: "If it seems too good to be true, it usually is."

Stick to the straight and narrow. A clear conscience is worth billions. There's no way to compute its high value! You sleep like a baby. Practically the second your head hits the pillow you're in peaceful dreamland. You stay there all night, wake up the next morning—refreshed! There's no haunted look in your eyes. You're in harmony with your highest self, your serenity knows no bounds. Isn't life delicious?

Jeremy loved to remind me of the first of Buddha's Four Noble Truths: life is suffering. I agree—to a point. A little suffering goes a long way.

Usually, if you do the right thing, you don't have to suffer, but occasional suffering is part of the package. Your only choice is to accept it with all the grace you can muster. Childbirth, for instance, is worth the pain. As are dental work and cosmetic surgery. Thank goodness my teeth are perfect. And I certainly don't need cosmetic surgery. But if I ever do, I won't hesitate to contact whoever Marian Colby's been using for the last decade.

I've been cursed with more than my share of enemies, all of whom had the morals of alley cats. Like Jonathan Kinder, they were masters of disguise who pretended in the beginning to care about me, wormed their way into my heart, massaged my ego, softened me up for the kill. In the end—often at the last minute—right prevailed. With right on your side, the forces of evil are always vanquished!

I've also struggled with deep and profound moral issues of my own. When I was fourteen I had a baby out of wedlock, and gave her up for adoption. In 1974 I had an abortion. In 1973 the Supreme Court of the United States had affirmed a woman's legal right to choose abortion. If they hadn't, I would have gone to Sweden, where the procedure was (and is) legal. If I hadn't been able to afford Sweden, I might have been victimized by some back-street butcher and died an agonizing death, and you would not be reading this book today. That's how certain I was then that for me to have a baby at that time was wrong.

I'm not "pro-abortion"! For heaven's sake, *nobody* is! I'm pro-choice, that's all.

My morals have been called into question quite often. I've already admitted I made terrible mistakes. Lying was my

Achilles' heel. I'm a gifted actress, so lies rolled off my tongue like honey.

Whoppers, innocent little social lies, even perjury were in my repertoire. For some reason, every false statement or action seemed justified at the time. Now, looking back, I can't help but marvel at the power of my denial. Often, it was only later, when the dust cleared, the battle was over, and the loser (me) condemned that I even realized I'd lied.

I've been broke, sick, lost, kidnapped, slammed into jails, mental institutions, and car wrecks, and once I spent what seemed like a week flat on my back in a damp catacomb, a marble statue pressed against my chest. Pinning me to the cold hard floor. I bring this up to illustrate I never broke a Commandment without suffering punishment of biblical proportions.

The road to hell is paved with good intentions. If your conscience cries out, stop in your tracks. Listen carefully to your inner voice. Find out what's wrong. Don't make another move until you figure out which principle of right thinking you're violating, and fix it.

Once you have morality squared away, take care not to impose your high standards on others. Tempting as it may be to warn loved ones who might wander from the moral path, resist! They'll never thank you.

Minding your own business is a crucial moral tenet. I can't understand why God forgot it when he gave Moses the Ten Commandments. My life is littered with nosy, interfering busybodies. They pry into my private affairs without shame. The only excitement in their dull lives is telling me how to live mine. I find them pathetic.

(1983; credit: GARY MILLER/ABC)

In disguise and on the run, from the time when lying was one of my best habits.

American morality springs from our earliest Puritan settlers. Bless their hearts, the pilgrims put up with a lot for the sake of freedom. They set high standards of honor. Truth, dignity, equality for everyone! Who could argue?

The loftiness of our national standards makes them hard to live up to. Luckily, escape clauses are built into our system. Nothing is more valued in America than individualism. In other words, nobody cares what your standards are. As long as you play by the rules you can't fail.

In keeping with my stoic position on morality, this chapter is rather spare. While I take pleasure in stating my own firmly held principles, I'm not really comfortable advising others on matters of conscience because, as Oscar Wilde wrote, "A man who moralizes is usually a hypocrite, and a woman who moralizes is invariably plain." Since I'm neither plain nor a hypocrite, let's proceed to my métier. . . .

# 5

## Romance

*W*orn out from tackling the weighty subject of morals, I had to have a nap and candlelit citrus salts bath before I was ready for the rejuvenating fun of discussing romance.

It permeates my soul. I never tire of the topic. Some cynic once wrote that romance is illusion. Phooey! It's as real and important as the air we breathe.

Romance is front burner in my life, always has been, always will be, and so should it be in yours. Honestly, what could be more important?

I'm the most romantic person I've ever met. First of all, I'm a magnet for rich, handsome, fascinating men. A smile, a fluttered eyelash, a brief moment of eye contact, *et voilà!* They're mine for life.

When you truly love yourself, your smile and your eyes

say everything. Eyes are windows to the soul. Keep them open and bright. Smile with confidence. Whatever you want will soon be yours.

The intimacy, tenderness, and love we yearn for is there, within ourselves, in our own hearts. It's the gift that keeps on giving. All we have to do is allow it free expression.

Many confuse romance with love or, worse, with sex. It is neither. Love is serious business. Sex is private. Romance is art.

In my opinion, at least half the day of the exceptional person who Has It ALL revolves around romance. It's there in everything *I* do. It begins in the morning. If my beloved and I spend the night in the same bed, I try to rise first, long before he does, so I can brush my teeth, make myself beautiful, and slide back into bed before he wakes up.

Sometimes I surprise him with breakfast in bed. Coral, my housekeeper of many years, fixes a tray to my exacting specifications and I carry it upstairs all by myself. I open the window for fresh air and the serenade of birdsong. Unless the blue jays are shrieking. That hurts my ears, so I close the windows and play a Mahler symphony instead. Once in a while I choose Bach. One of my husbands (I'll let you guess which) preferred Sousa.

Music enhances whatever mood you want to create. So do flowers. Aroma therapists tell us lavender and the scent of cedar promote romance, but I find most fragrant blooms do the job. Roses, gardenias, jasmine, and eucalyptus turn a ho-hum bedroom into a boudoir.

Massage is an elemental tool of romance. It relaxes the

body and spirit. It's an art form that requires no formal education. Simply anoint your palms and fingertips with aromatic oils and do unto the other what you would like done to you and vice versa.

Your bedroom is a sanctuary, a retreat that reflects the peaceful, self-loving inner you. Real flowers, soft lighting, fine fabrics define the décor. The focal point of your haven is the bed itself. Make it the stuff of which dreams are made, the best that money can buy.

Never scrimp on linens. Sheets, feather-light duvets, pillows, towels, etc., are luxury items worthy of major investment. To slide squeaky-clean between the cool satin sheets of a freshly made bed is an exquisitely romantic pleasure that never grows old.

Massive storage space is a must. You'll need separate closets for lingerie, evening clothes, outerwear, perhaps a whole room just for shoes. Color or fabric coordination helps keep things organized. Nothing reflects your romantic heart more than your wardrobe, so a spacious dressing room is a luxury a person who Has It ALL can afford.

The international *crème de la crème* of fashion designers inject romance into every creation they offer. Even the most austere little black dress becomes a romantic frock by adding a touch of whimsy—any bauble from Cartier, Tiffany, or Harry Winston will suffice.

Clothes should appeal to all senses. No detail is too small to consider. The lines of a suit or the texture of a sweater can make all the difference. Comfort counts. The better you feel, the better you look.

When building a wardrobe, remember that only a wedding gown is constructed to look beautiful from the back, so be careful. You're observed from behind as often as face to face. In fashion as in everything else, it pays to watch your back.

Food has age-old romantic associations. "The way to a man's heart is through his stomach" rings true, but thankfully studying gourmet cooking or fixing his mother's famous pot roast every Wednesday night with your own two hands is not required. That's what kitchen staff is for, and whoever founded the institution of takeout should be canonized.

The important thing is that every meal consumed with your beloved should be a feast. Even if nothing passes your lips but a sip of grapefruit juice and a nibble of whole-grain toast, the breaking of bread together is fraught with intimacy. Treat each repast as a banquet.

Anticipation heightens enjoyment of any activity, especially romance. Tuck notes in pockets and briefcases, be eloquent about how much you look forward to being together. Write poems if you can. Borrow from the classics if you must. Pin a spray of rosemary to your beloved's lapel. Rosemary is for remembrance.

The element of surprise also romanticizes a relationship. Let your beloved learn to expect the unexpected. Boring predictability is the enemy of love.

Gifts are a delightful necessity. Giving and/or receiving a love token can make someone's day. A cabochon ruby surrounded by diamonds is guaranteed to lift spirits. A fast

(New Orleans,1981; credit: ABC)

The Belle of New Orleans on a photo shoot!

sports car or two weeks in the Caribbean is also heartwarming. Remember, it's the thought that counts.

Contentment plays a part in every great romance. Drama and ecstasy are important, but contentment is the foundation on which romance thrives. It can only be achieved when love is real. Never take it for granted. And never—ever—allow it to become boring.

Be open to adventure. Nothing creates a climate for romance better than setting out on a quest. Never be afraid to take risks. I've been at death's door more than once, only to be rescued by a swashbuckler. As every woman who's ever

59

been rescued by one knows, these reckless, swaggering, dare-devil pirates are practically irresistible.

Swashbucklers come in all sizes, shapes, colors, and religious preferences. This is where your self-loving tolerance of others come in handy!

A man doesn't have to look like a mythical hero to be one. Mike Roy, one of the great loves of my life and unbilled coauthor of my first book, *Raising Kane*, wore glasses. Dimitri Marick has a scar, Jackson Montgomery has a tattoo, and Adam Chandler has wicked eyes.

Also, you don't have to be tied to the railroad tracks with an express train less than half a mile away to need rescuing. Men come in handy for much more than that. How do you find these rugged buccaneers? You needn't bother! When you love yourself and Have It ALL, they find you.

Never turn down an opportunity to travel. Adventure flourishes in exotic locales. This means paying strict attention to mind-numbing details like keeping your passport current.

You can travel to our closest neighbors (Canada, Mexico, and most Caribbean nations) with only a photo ID and a voter registration card. But world-renowned romantic destinations like France, Tibet, Hungary, Moscow, New Guinea, and Grindlewald, Switzerland, require passports. Some picky governments even insist on visas! This odious bureaucratic red-tape–laden task is best assigned to a private secretary or factotum.

Dreams are an ideal way to jump start your romantic life. Both daydreams and night dreams are rich fodder for the heart. Arrange plenty of time in your schedule to enjoy them.

Unstructured daydreams are my personal first choice. Seers and gurus would perhaps call it meditating. Allowing your thoughts to drift aimlessly can be very spiritual. Fantasy in which I am the star refreshes my body and invigorates my soul.

Daydreaming is a portable pleasure. You can do it anywhere! Backseats of stretch limos, bubble baths, and sandy beaches are perfect places to indulge, but so are campfires, helicopters, anyplace you feel the inclination.

Treat yourself. Make it happen! Dreams *do* come true.

Next to your bed, a hope chest is the most romantic piece of furniture you can own. You don't have to be single to have one. A hope chest should be a thing of beauty and a joy forever. In other words, a work of art. You wouldn't store treasure in anything less.

My hope chest was a gift from my mother. It's cedar, of course, a priceless antique. In it, I keep souvenirs: old letters, photographs, locks of hair, silver teething rings, baby cups, my great-grandmother's Bible, my daughter Bianca's christening gown, pressed flowers, Mother's wedding ring, mothballs, and a host of other cherished mementos of my full and satisfying life.

Next to my hope chest, the thing I love most is my secret garden. Wherever I live, I pick a beautiful spot outdoors, in easy reach of the house, to call my own. At Wildwind, a walled herb garden with roses in the center and each of the four corners fits the bill. A white marble bench on the north (shady) side provides seating. Here at Linden House, it's the wisteria arbor. In the spring, there's a glorious drift of purple flowers. I sit on a teak glider and let my imagination—like the butterflies—take flight.

Spring is the natural season of romance. Life is reborn! Every season of the year should be chock-full of loving moments, but spring is when even the grouchiest bear has to admit life is grand. Christmas has the same effect. Without exception, *every* holiday is reason to celebrate!

Which is precisely why you shouldn't limit yourself to tradition! Adopt other cultures' holidays. Whenever one sounds attractive, embrace it as your own! Invent your own fiesta. Nobody's calendar is too crowded. I never let Bastille Day go by without fireworks. *Vive la France!* Ditto Chinese New Year. I pride myself on being ecumenical.

Curiosity is the fast track to romance. Whatever engages you, tweaks your fancy, pursue! She who hesitates to expand her knowledge is doomed. Read. The more you read, the more you understand. Asking a question, then unearthing the answer yourself is a key to enlightenment.

Romance is Zen-ish. It crops up when it pleases, sometimes in the most outlandish places! I'll never forget an intense encounter—with a barrister who shall remain nameless—fully clothed, on a mildewed green felt pool table in the saloon of a desert ghost town. Even though I'd been bitten by a rattlesnake, it was heaven! Lightning can—and will—strike anywhere.

Now that we've chatted about delightful ways to welcome

romance, create proper moods, and prepare ourselves for the occasion, it's time to discuss danger.

When you give free rein to your romantic self, you'll never want to live any other way. With love as your guiding force, you're always protected. But romance has many enemies, so don't lose your edge. Be alert!

Gloom and depression can wipe out happiness faster than a flash flood. If you suffer from any debilitating mental condition that saps your joy, see a shrink! Get therapy. Just thinking about the horrible ickiness of depression makes my skin crawl.

Do whatever has to be done to restore your cheerful mood. Go for a swim, call your best friend, have a facial and a pedicure. Don't wallow in misery. Never inflict tears on a loved one, even by accident. Where's the appeal in red eyes and wet face? There are exceptions, but generally, a person who Has It ALL hates to cry.

Jealousy kills romance. This ugly affliction is far too common. I've attracted many jealous admirers over the years, people who pretend to care, but secretly envy me because I Have It ALL. I speak my mind. I get what I want, and I make it look easy. Of course it's not easy. You wouldn't need this book if it were! Jealous people don't want to love you. They want to own you.

Control freaks are everywhere. Adam Chandler is probably the best example among my former husbands. I know he won't mind if I say it because, bless his wizened little heart, Adam doesn't deny his major character flaws. Perhaps that explains why I married him twice. Honesty doesn't *cancel out* character flaws, but it does make a difference.

The notion of jealousy frankly bewilders me. I mean, I understand why people are jealous of me. But even so, why spoil a perfectly lovely day by allowing that green-eyed monster to rear its nasty head? I haven't got a jealous bone in my body, thank goodness.

I have, however, tried to control a relationship or two, and the result was always disastrous. My marriage to sweet Tom Cudahy best illustrates how I tried—unsuccessfully, of course!—to mold an adorable hunk into my immature vision of what a husband should be. What a disaster. Tom, darling, if you read this: I apologize.

Another good example of a death knell to romance is dishonesty. Every religion preaches honesty. Dimitri destroyed our marriage with lies. Every broken Commandment has a negative impact on romance, but lies are especially deadly. Be truthful! Turn away from lies and liars. You won't regret it.

Poor hygiene is a topic I cannot even bear to discuss, save to say it's totally taboo for romantics! You wouldn't fly to the moon on a roach-infested rocket, would you? Treat your body like the sacred machine it is. Fuel it, keep it clean, and oil its parts regularly.

Selfishness is also banned and the very essence of romance is not being self-conscious! Prethinking destroys spontaneity. Save your personal agenda for work situations. The more other-oriented you are in your private life, the better. As I've pointed out before, the more you give, the more you get.

My first wedding to Adam Chandler.

I've also already pointed out the evils of intolerance. A romantic mood will fizzle at the merest hint of the noxious presence of prejudice. Once I made the gross error of keeping company with a courtly foreign man, now dead, named Lars Bogard. I was young, so for a while I was charmed by his urbane wit and sophisticated lifestyle. Then I discovered, to my horror, he was a Nazi! Ugh! As you can imagine, it took a long time to forgive myself.

Illness eviscerates romance. When I fell from that infamous scaffolding, injured my back, pain became my constant companion. Pain took over my head, threw out everything else, made me its slave. There was no room for other feelings, only pain.

Guard yourself and your loved ones. Nothing takes the place of a healthy mind in a healthy body.

Embrace romance! Every day, in every way.

Consider your life an angel food cake. Let romance be the frosting. Whipped cream and strawberries, meringue and apricot jam are nice toppings. A new embellishment several times a day is even nicer. As my friend Opal Cortlandt, another romantic, would say, "Go hog wild!"

# 6

# Marriage and Divorce

$\mathcal{I}$ believe in marriage. With all my heart and soul. Incongruous as it may seem for a person with my history, happily ever after is what I'm all about. In spite of overwhelming evidence to the contrary, my faith in enduring true love never wavers.

Not that I don't adore being single; I do! Whatever label society hands me—single, married, divorced—I go at it full-throttle. I never do anything halfway. I love my independence, my freedom to date every handsome, fascinating man who appeals to me. But someday—soon, probably, if I haven't already met him—the special man I'm waiting for will show up and change everything!

Marriage to the right partner is paradise on earth.

The bliss begins with a proposal. In the olden days, only the man was allowed to ask. Now it's an even field. Whoever pops the question has the responsibility to make it the most romantic proposal ever offered. Speak from the heart. Explain why you can't live without your beloved. Recite poetry. Wear a garland of flowers in your hair. Release white doves from wicker baskets. Beg for the honor of his or her hand on bended knee if you want.

Few proposals of marriage are sealed without the *pièce de résistance*, the engagement ring. An engagement ring is an important symbol, almost as important as a wedding ring. It's a sign of betrothal. A sort of down payment. The shape—a circle—represents infinity. The foreverness of love! If I had to choose a ring today, I'd pick a traditional six-carat, square-cut diamond in a Tiffany setting—or a sapphire surrounded by starbursts of emeralds—or a heart-shaped ruby with diamond baguettes—or—never mind! The design doesn't matter. Neither does how much it costs. One of the best proposals I ever accepted was sealed when he slipped a cigar band on the third finger of my left hand.

If you marry young, when only the paltriest of diamonds can be squeezed into your budget, fret not. Engagement rings are like all major purchases. They need to be upgraded regularly. Yearly trade-ins are not excessive.

As soon as you're sure there's a ring in your future, set up those weekly manicure appointments! Nothing is less attractive than a sparkling new ring on a dry, chapped finger with a broken nail. Wait until after you're married to wash dishes, use harsh cleansers, or type.

There's no better occasion for a party than an engagement. The guests get in line to congratulate the groom-to-be and offer the bride-to-be best wishes! Back when men did all the asking, the bride's parents were the hosts, but now—anything goes. When it comes to modern American marriage rituals, the rules are: There are no rules.

Engagement parties (especially mine) no longer are limited to white as a color scheme, although masses of white roses and baby's-breath tied with white satin ribbons are always in good taste. Well-behaved children are welcome in their Sunday best. Plenty of Champagne and sparkling water should be available for toasts. A wedding or engagement party without toasts is unthinkable!

As soon as the troth is plighted, it's time to make the formal announcement. If you don't have a press secretary, simply send a black and white portrait of the bride along with all relevant information on the happy couple to the newspaper. Annoyingly, some newspapers will print either an engagement announcement or a wedding announcement, but not both. This is extremely selfish on their part, and calls for a letter-to-the-editor protesting the policy. Politely suggest they quit publishing all that boring bad news and give readers more pictures of brides!

After the party and the announcement, it's time for the showers! Luncheons or teas with cucumber and watercress sandwiches, crumpets and scones, delicate frosted pastries to match the pastel dresses and festive hats of the guests are the most fun. Friends of the bride gather with gaily wrapped gifts to stock her lingerie closet or linen chest. Ribbons and bows are threaded through a paper plate to make a charming bouquet for the stand-in bride at the wedding rehearsal.

A fairly recent innovation is the coed shower, and these are fun, too! Usually, a stronger beverage than tea is served, and off-color jokes might be told. Every groom should have at least one prenuptial shower.

The wedding party needs to be carefully chosen. After all, you'll be looking at photographs of the maid-of-honor and best man for the rest of your life, so make sure you like whomever you pick. Photogenic quality might be considered as well. If the bride or the groom is a parent, include the children in the wedding party.

Don't be tied to tradition. If you want a man-of-honor or a best woman, go ahead! Be daring! I personally draw the line at pets, but some of my friends have had animals in their wedding parties.

Special attention should be paid to the mother of the bride. Hers is the second most important gown after the bride's. The mother of the groom also ranks high. Corsages, flattering toasts to their child-rearing skills, choice tidbits from the hors d'oeuvres tray, nothing is too good for these gallant women.

The father of the bride deserves attention. His job is to pay for the wedding. Thankfully, this custom hasn't yet gone out of style.

Before things go much further, the person who plans to Have It ALL sits down and signs a prenuptial agreement. Planning for the divorce before the bouquet is tossed is not romantic. Prenups are cynical and, worse, coldhearted, but they are practical. You owe it to yourself to protect any property you bring into a marriage. Believe me, every time I didn't

Mother and Bianca at my wedding to Dimitri.

sign one, I was sorry. Fear not. If his, or her, love is true, he, or she, will *want* to protect your future.

Some things I'll include in my next prenup are: Whoever breaks the wedding vows pays all the legal fees. If both are guilty, both pay. Nobody can sue for alimony. Nobody can write a book, film script, or television series about the marriage if it fails. These are only a few ideas. I'm sure my lawyer will have more.

Now that we've covered all bases, we can plan the ceremony!

The best marriages are performed by ordained clergy in a house of worship. If that's not an option, home will do. Garden weddings are lovely unless it rains, and yachts, beaches, justice-of-the-peace offices, Las Vegas chapels, judge's chambers, and mountaintops are also acceptable. A ship's captain can pronounce you husband and wife on the high seas.

The couple who Has It ALL writes their own vows. When you're in love, eloquence flows from your pen like water over Niagara Falls. Harness your energy! Write vows only Shakespeare could equal. You can do it. I have, many times.

Never—ever—take a vow you don't intend to keep. This is like asking to be thrown into a pit filled with hungry lions. Marriage vows are sacred. Break them, and fate will punish you, mark my words. I'm living proof.

The most crucial thing to promise your mate is honesty. More marriages are killed by lies than any other cause. It's so sad. If you ask me, dishonest people—such as my most recent ex—should do the human race a favor and refrain from marriage and reproduction altogether. If they'd just do that one little thing, we could wipe out liars in one generation.

A wedding gown is the most romantic dress you'll ever wear. I buy all of mine from world-class designers, but you might be lucky enough to inherit one. Or perhaps you can sew. In any event, whether it's an elegant peau-de-soie sheath designed by Yvette Valjean or miles of hoop-skirted ruffled satin created by your grandmother, it should be perfect in every respect.

I lean toward white or off-white as a color choice, but once I made a statement of sorts by marrying Adam in black from head to toe. As I recall, Nina Cortlandt was stunning in emerald green the fourth time she became Mrs. Cliff Warner, and my mother wore mauve when she married Dr. Tyler. Whatever color makes you feel like the most glorious bride who ever said "I do" is the one to choose.

The veil is my favorite element of the outfit. I like floor-length clouds of white netting embroidered with seed pearls and wispy peek-a-boo screens attached to hats. I like beaded headbands and Belgian lace. I like it all! To me, the most romantic moment of the ceremony is when the groom lifts the veil and kisses the bride. Perhaps this is why I keep repeating that walk to the altar.

Lots of pre-wedding time needs to be set aside for trousseau-shopping. A trousseau is the wardrobe a bride brings to her marriage, and it must be fabulous! You can go to the stores on your own, or have the designers come to you. Every trousseau should include peignoirs, negligees, nightgowns, bed jackets, camisoles, etc., as well as dresses, gowns, casual and outerwear. Spare no expense!

Meanwhile, prepare to receive more gifts. Specifically, something old, something new, something borrowed, and something blue. This cherished convention takes place as the bride dresses for the ceremony. It's a wonderful opportunity for friends to be generous.

Depending on the type of wedding, receptions can be formal or informal. I tend toward formal, with old-fashioned receiving lines, toasts to the bride, dancing. I thrill to the whole cake-cutting, bouquet-tossing lark of it! Every wedding should be a pageant.

For centuries, guests pelted brides and grooms with rice as they left the church or reception. For the last decade or so, that ancient fertility ritual is no longer practiced. It's politically incorrect. Birds ate the rice, got bloated, and died or something. Now whatever you pelt the happy couple with must be biodegradable. Birdseed is thoughtful. Bubble blowing can be an attractive way to send the bride and groom on their way.

Honeymoons are another delightful benefit of the marriage package. The euphoric joy of the first two to six weeks of a marriage should be experienced in an exotic location with a full staff at your beck and call. A *discreet* staff. The kind who blend with the woodwork. Newlyweds need privacy. Make your honeymoon the happiest, most memorable trip you ever take because when you Have It ALL, the honeymoon never ends!

Once the hoopla of parties, showers, ceremonies, recep-

Tom Cudahy and me on our honeymoon in the Virgin Islands.

tions and honeymoon is over, and, of course, after you sign the thank-you notes your social secretary writes and mails, the marriage starts in earnest. Now the real work begins.

The secret to a long and happy union is commitment. If you and your partner follow the program laid out in this book, I guarantee you'll be together until death do you part. That prenuptial agreement you signed will gather cobwebs in your safe deposit box. In fact, seventy-five years from now, I'll help you celebrate your diamond wedding anniversary.

Sadly, half of all American marriages end in divorce. This heartbreaking legal action begins when one or the other or occasionally *both* partners break the commitment. I hope it goes without saying that the one who breaks the commitment doesn't Have It ALL.

However—things happen. No-fault divorce laws make it possible to dissolve a marriage on the flimsiest grounds of "incompatibility" or "irreconcilable differences," but people who Have It ALL never go to court over petty issues like those.

Adultery blows up our marriages. Lying, cheating, betraying spouses make up their minds *not* to Have It ALL, to be driven by greed, lust, or pride, and we have no choice but to rip them out of our lives. We don't waste any time crying about it, either. We call a lawyer.

Some lawyers claim marriage is a contract, and contracts are made to be broken. We know better. Marriage is a holy vow we don't take unless we're 100 percent prepared to keep it. Period. But we can't speak for our spouse. If we're betrayed by that spouse and a friend, relative, or sister-in-law, all bets are off. We cut our losses, get the heck out of Dodge.

This requires hiring the best legal guns in the business, the ones who write books and appear on talk shows, the kind who love to fight dirty. We only know how to fight fair, so we leave everything up to him or her.

As the aggrieved party, we demand only our rights. We resist the urge to take the cheater to the cleaners, insist on prompt payment of our half of community property as outlined in the prenuptial agreement, and exit the courtroom with dignity. If we're really smart, we let lawyers represent us, never even go near the courthouse. Why should we? We're above it.

They say life's most stressful events are death, divorce, moving, and getting fired. The person who Has It ALL will suffer emotional strain going through a divorce, but we'll always find a positive spin. Laugh and the world laughs with you; cry and you cry alone.

Sometimes an unspeakable marriage can end without the torture of divorce. A clever attorney can arrange an annulment. Fraud, duress, mental incompetency, and impotence are grounds for annulment in many states. It also helps if the marriage isn't consummated.

A vicious, no-holds-barred divorce is to be avoided at all costs. Take my word for it. A fight to the death leaves everyone wounded. Scars heal slowly. If children are involved, the damage to them is immense, almost unforgivable.

Custody battles harm everyone. Often they're about one parent wanting to control or manipulate the other. Rarely are they about what's best for the child. A tip from my personal file: Never trust an attorney to perjure himself. Making this error cost me custody of Bianca. In my opinion, all children belong with their mothers, but some judges don't agree with me. Whoever wins custody should encourage liberal visitation by the other parent.

Should you find yourself in the doldrums over a divorce, don't give in. Take action! Call your travel agent, fly to Bali for a week in the sun, or redecorate your house. Throw a divorce shower for yourself, encourage your friends to cheer you up with presents.

Divorce is the end of a dream, yes, but it's also the beginning of new, exciting challenges. When you Have It ALL, the future is bright, the here and now is all that counts.

In summary, I have one word to say about marriage. Yes! And one word to say about divorce. No! I hope that's clear.

# 7

*Motherhood*

*A* Jewish proverb I love goes something like: God could not be everywhere, and therefore made mothers. Motherhood is a life-affirming, life-changing experience. No offense to fathers, but motherhood is, in the vernacular of my childhood, where it's at. For sure.

Scholars say that before Judaism, Christianity, Islam—even before the pantheon of Greek and Roman gods—our ancestors worshipped a deity known as the Earth Mother. With her consort, the Sun, she was in charge of the seasons, the fertility of plants and animals, life as we know it.

Eventually, marauding male-dominated tribes from some barbaric land invaded, burned, pillaged, raped, and conquered our gentle prehistoric foremothers, imposed their brutal patriarchal system, and thus began the slow decline of Western civilization.

If mothers were still in charge, we wouldn't have all our modern problems, including nuclear proliferation. Oh, well. It's a waste of time to worry about the past; learn from it instead!

Motherhood is a sacred institution. Nothing is purer or more holy than the bond between mother and child. My eyes well with tears just thinking about the first time I held my daughter Bianca in my arms. I'll never forget the flow of love I felt as her tiny heart beat against mine.

Every woman knows you can tell a lot about a man by the way he treats his mother. If he doesn't honor her, recall the Ten Commandments. Cross him off!

Men should also be respectful and kind to the mothers of their own children, whether or not they're divorced. That's how sacred motherhood is, in my opinion.

You might find it odd that a woman who, at fourteen, gave up a child for adoption, had an abortion before she was twenty, and, later, lost custody of her only legal daughter could speak so reverently of sacred motherhood. If you do find it strange, you need to immediately reread the earlier chapters. I told you, a person who Has It ALL comes to terms with life's disappointments, not to mention its challenges.

Fate hasn't always dealt kindly with me. Evil opportunists spread rumors and lies, an unprincipled press prints their filthy fabrications. The truth is, I'm as gifted at motherhood as I am at everything else. If that sounds immodest, too bad. As my friend Trevor Dillon, a decorated Vietnam veteran, says, "If you don't toot your own horn someone'll come along and use it for a relief tube."

Travis and I christen our precious Bianca.

A woman who wants to Have It ALL must carefully consider her reproductive options. Not everyone is cut out to excel at raising children. I wouldn't be giving you the whole story if I failed to note pregnancy can be tedious, dangerous, and woefully uncomfortable. You may never regain your figure or lose your stretch marks. Childbirth can be agony. And that's just the beginning.

If changing diapers, wiping spit-up off your ball gown, and leaving the party early to take a shrieking baby to the doctor doesn't appeal to you, look out. Naturally you'll have nurses and nannies to help, but believe me, even the most glamorous mommy deals with diapers. You can't avoid them. Like taxes, they're inescapable—and unpleasant.

There's nothing wrong with choosing not to reproduce! Some of my best friends are barren. Overpopulation is a problem worldwide. In China, the government only allows couples to have one child! Imagine living in a country where the choice isn't yours. God bless America.

What's bad—and will absolutely derail your quest to Have It ALL—is having a baby and not wanting it; or vice versa, wanting one and not having it. It's sad when that happens, but when it does, adoption is the answer!

Adoption can be time-consuming and far from easy, but do not be tempted to take shortcuts! As I recently told one of my staff, "Finders-keepers does *not* apply to babies." Even if a child is left on your doorstep like a cherubic bouquet, make every attempt to legally adopt the little darling. Few of us can fake trips to Eastern Europe and foreign adoptions and get away with it.

If you opt not to reproduce, be sure you have a cat or a dog, a niece or a nephew, whatever, upon whom to lavish your love. After all, love is our reason for being here, it's all there is.

Bear in mind that the challenge of motherhood is enormous and never-ending, but the rewards are worth the effort. If you decide this is the route for you, good luck!

You'll need patience. Patience in vast quantities. So much patience that you'll be sick of the concept long before the child is potty-trained. Patience is not a quality we're born with. We have to learn. Sadly, often the hard way.

If your patience skills are not up to par, don't worry. Your children will teach you. My sainted mother claimed I taught her everything she knew. I'm sure I did. By the time I was a teenager, I knew everything!

Every mom is a working mom. The juggling acts we perform are monumental! There's always more work to do than there's time for, but somehow, we make it happen. Being organized helps. Make a schedule and make your staff stick to it! But keep it flexible because motherhood, like everything else worth having, is full of surprises.

Don't expect fairy-tale children. Be realistic! Even my precious daughter Bianca hasn't had smooth sailing. She was the eensiest bit too fond of fire as a toddler, and stubbornness appears to be a personality trait she inherited from me. My daughter has strong opinions that don't always agree with mine, but I respect them. Keep all your insurance policies—home and health—up to date! Above all, allow your child to be herself. Or himself. Love them exactly the way they are, the same way you want them to love you.

Discipline counts. Be firm. Let your precious angels know where you stand. Make sensible rules, and insist they be followed. Explain why you insist on high standards. Try to make them listen. When you love yourself and take responsibility for everything you say and do, you teach by example. Children love their parents, and naturally want to be like them.

Have fun with your offspring! Play games together, develop hobbies the whole family can enjoy. Bianca loves horses. I, however, prefer transportation with engines, but I don't let that stop me. I ride with my daughter. I've even been brave

This was my mother's favorite, kept in a silver frame on her dresser.

enough to give a horse an apple. Who knows, perhaps some-day I'll actually groom one.

Motherhood is the only job for which there's no training. OJT (On the Job Training) is all most of us get. We pick up information from relatives, books, magazines. Sometimes it seems as if every know-it-all on the planet wants to give us advice. So listen, it won't hurt you. Then make up your own mind.

If we were lucky enough to be raised by a good mother ourselves, how can we misstep? The answer is, by breaking the Ten Commandments or the Golden Rule. That's how I lost custody of Bianca.

Some may wonder how I survived the tragic circum-stances surrounding each of my conception experiences, much less manage to be so gung-ho about motherhood. I could have been bitter. Or blamed others (correctly, since none of the tragedies was my fault). Instead of bewailing my fate, I choose to accept, make the best of it!

Children are our most valuable natural resource. Society's most vulnerable, they have the least rights. Therefore it's up to us—every one of us—to protect children. All children. Not just our own.

I could have blamed my mother because she allowed me to visit my father in California, where I was raped and impregnated by one of his so-called friends when I was four-teen. I could have spent hundreds of thousands of dollars, thousands of hours in therapy pinning the blame on her, but where would that get me? It wasn't her fault! It was the fault of that nasty Richard Fields and nobody else.

Later, I accidentally thought Dimitri was Richard Fields and stabbed him, a foolish act with consequences that included losing everything I valued most. I dredge up these dreadful memories only to emphasize the depths from which a person who truly loves herself can rise.

Little things mean a lot to mothers. A dandelion presented by a small, chubby hand is as charming as an armful of long-stemmed American Beauty roses. Handmade cards, drawings, camp projects, all are major keepsakes. A gift from your child is a gift from the heart. Treasure each and every one. One of my most prized possessions is a powder-blue and buff lanyard key chain Bianca wove for me in summer camp.

Motherhood fosters sisterhood. It begins during pregnancy. Like magic, you start noticing other women in a new, more favorable light. Having a baby brings women together, reminds us of the ways we're alike, gives us a fresh feeling of connectedness. Even though some of these women might later betray you, savor the present. You cannot fear the future.

The woman who Has It ALL succeeds as a mother because she always does her best. She regards her job as a holy calling, to be there for her offspring, listen to their troubles, guide them, gently nudge them into a healthy adulthood where they, too, can Have It ALL.

It's like a dynasty! If the entire planet would just follow these rudimentary principles, think what a paradise we could create. The Garden of Eden, Part II. Figure it out, and pass it on. The hand that rocks the cradle rules the world.

Nobody remains a child forever. When children grow up and if they ever leave home (or, worse, you lose custody) you will experience the dreaded "empty nest" syndrome. My mother, who was practically faultless, suffered painfully when I moved out. For years, she kept my bedroom as a shrine.

My own heartache started the day I lost Bianca to her father, an excruciating fact I'm forced to live with every day. Nevertheless, Travis and I are respectful of each other. We're exceedingly civil, polite for the sake of our daughter. If you're a divorced parent, your obligation is to maintain cordial relations with your ex-spouse no matter how much you want to rip his—or her—face off with your bare hands.

Bianca has two loving homes. She spends summers and vacations with me in Pine Valley, and goes to school with her father and the woman he married in Seattle. I fly out west to visit as often as I can. I maintain an 800 number so she can call any time of the day or night. We talk on the phone for hours at a time.

The sublime closeness and mother/daughter rapport I enjoy with my child is proof of my spiritual beliefs: Everything happens the way it's supposed to and always turns out for the best.

As I said, regaining your perfect figure after childbirth can be daunting—if not downright impossible. Smooth the way back to svelte by making your workout, your diet, your new life of being on-call twenty-four hours a day, at the utter mercy of a squalling infant, a life of joy! Just because poets don't write sonnets about sit-ups, salad, and diaper rash doesn't mean they're not worthy. They are!

Educating a young person can be very expensive. Don't forget to set aside gobs of money for this purpose when you make your investments. Nothing is more crucial to a young person's development than education.

I myself am completely self-taught. Formal education bored me senseless. My fellow students were light-years behind me in both social and intellectual achievement (this sounds like bragging, but isn't since it was fact!). High school was all I could force myself to complete.

My dream is for Bianca to go to college. Harvard would be my first choice since the city of Cambridge, Massachusetts, where the university is located, has everything. I adore Cambridge! In fact, one of my proudest moments and fondest memories is the award I was given by Harvard's Hasty Pudding Club. Maybe someday they'll give me an honorary degree. If not, when I'm old I'll enroll, study something esoteric like Egyptology, just for the fun of it.

Scientists point out procreation is our biological purpose on earth. We're here to reproduce ourselves, and, ultimately, our species. What could be more humbling or profound? If by our own free will we elect to fulfill our purpose, how could we give any less than our best?

Most of the women I admire most are mothers. My friends Opal Cortlandt, Ruth Martin, and Janet Green are shining examples of what mothers should be. Each would lay down her life for her child, fight to the death in defense of her cubs.

Motherhood is the crown jewel of family values. If your mother's still alive and you haven't given her flowers lately,

(1980; credit: ANN LIMONGELLO/ABC)

My brother Mark, my mother, me, and Mike Roy, coauthor of *Raising Kane*.

what are you waiting for? Let her know how much you appreciate her. On your birthday send *her* a gift! Write her a letter. Say how grateful you are for all she's done for you and the valuable lessons she's taught you.

If you have children yourself, track them down right now and give them a hug. Express your love! Tell them how much they mean to you! Nobody ever hears it too often.

# 8

*Forgiveness*

*F*orgiveness earns a chapter of its own because without it, you're lost, without hope of ever Having It ALL. It's a sad but certain truism, dear readers. There is no true peace without forgiveness.

Theology teaches us to love our neighbor as ourself, forgive our enemies as we expect to be forgiven. Secular philosophers are more succinct. "Forgiveness is better than revenge," the ancient (and warlike) Greeks admitted, and heaven knows they were right.

If life were perfect, there would be no conflict. No war, pestilence, floods, or fire. No widows, no orphans, no poverty. No one would ever lie or cheat. But life isn't perfect. There's a scoundrel lurking behind every potted palm, and you are their target.

Get used to it.

You're not paranoid; if you Have It ALL, people *really are* out to get you. Jealous, lazy wannabes lust after what you have, and, believe me, they're willing to lie, cheat, and steal to snatch it away from you. It's distressing, but you must accept this law of the jungle as a fact of life, dear readers, and prepare for even worse: Whatever the wretches do, whether or not you have legal recourse, you have to forgive them.

It's awful, isn't it? But don't say I didn't warn you! I told you right away, in the very beginning, that nothing worth having comes easy.

Readying your heart for forgiveness is backbreaking work. When someone betrays you, you wouldn't be human if you weren't enraged.

Never mind for the moment the emotional cost of enragement. Consider the physical toll. The hot blood pounding through your veins, the itchy trigger finger, the urge to kill—the stress on your body is horrible! It makes my head hurt just to think about how fury can deplete precious positive energy. Anger—even righteous anger!—can blow us off the map.

Feel your righteous anger, recognize it as a negative thing, and get rid of it. As fast and efficiently as possible. Forgive!

Luckily, you don't have to shoulder the burden alone. You can give your anger to your Higher Power and ask for the strength to forgive in return. Be humble. A humble heart can move mountains.

Some of my worst enemies eventually became friends, thanks to forgiveness. Brooke English is a textbook example. We were at bitter odds for years. We clashed over her chronic

(1981; credit: ABC)

The New Orleans Saints named me their favorite majorette.

jealousy, men, careers, civic issues, the women's movement—we couldn't agree on one single thing!

Poor Brooke was driven to compete with me on every level and, of course, destined to fail. Once we were held hostage together by revolutionaries in South America, and all we did was fight! I'm ashamed to admit there were actually times when we pulled hair, even tried to scratch each other's eyes out. I blush just remembering. Now Brooke and I are almost bosom buddies.

Janet Green was Public Enemy Number One in Pine Valley for eons. In loyal sympathy with my friend, Trevor Dillon, I built up a lot of resentment toward Janet. I took at face value reports of her crimes. Through a tangle of happenstance involving the vile drug pusher, Jonathan Kinder,

Palmer Cortlandt and I share a love for the sea.

Janet and I became allies, then friends. Forgiving her was simple. Even though she's done terrible things, deep down Janet Green is a warm, loving person.

Palmer, Adam, Opal, Tad, Dimitri, Edmund, Maria, Jackson—even Stuart Chandler, who wouldn't hurt a fly, all were my enemies at one time, now forgiven.

Forgiveness, of course, is the cornerstone not only of the world's great religions, but, more importantly, of my own hard-won serenity.

A favorite slogan at the Betty Ford Center is "Forgiveness is giving up on the idea that the past could have had different results." It's so true! Once you stop blaming others for messing up your life, you can forgive them, and get on with the important business of Having It ALL!

It is more important to understand than to be understood. I resisted learning that lesson so diligently I still have scars. They ache when it rains. An open mind is the best route to understanding. Try to see the other person's point of view. Even if their point of view is obviously wrong, you can at least find out why.

I'm no biblical scholar, but several years ago I noticed that what is now my favorite verse (1 Corinthians 13:13) had undergone a transformation. What used to be, "And now abideth faith, hope, charity, these three; but the greatest of these is charity" has become "And now abideth faith, hope, love, these three; but the greatest of these is love." Charity and love the same thing?! For me, it was a spiritual revelation. Love is the only thing that lasts.

How do you forgive someone who's harmed you? First,

you have to be willing. Think how lighthearted you'll feel when you unload that burden of anger you've carried so long. Imagine the feeling of freedom you'll have. Even if the person who harmed you doesn't *want* your forgiveness, you can still give it.

Next you have to train yourself to do what lawyers do. Try to look at things from both sides. You already know how extenuating circumstances can lead to disaster, so be charitable. Assume the person who harmed you did so without premeditation. Think of it as a cosmic accident.

If there's someone in your life whose crimes against you were deliberate, premeditated, evil beyond the pale—I'm sorry, but you still have to forgive them. That's right. A blanket pardon is required. You cannot let hatred consume you.

Some transgressions are so wicked you may think they're impossible to forgive. I understand. In addition to the common litany of lies and theft, I've had to forgive people for such disgusting crimes as murder, rape, child molesting, arson, and all types of vicious hate crimes.

If I can do it, so can you.

The benefits of forgiveness are wide and far-reaching. Besides the shimmering, iridescent halo you earn, you'll sleep better. Like a clear conscience, forgiveness is the elixir of sweet dreams.

It will also heal your inner pain. When you let go of grudges, your mind is swept clean. Light shines in new corners. It's like being reborn. Remember: Nothing can hurt you unless you let it.

Successful and satisfying romantic relationships can't

exist without forgiveness. How could they? Everyone's human. Besides, making up is fun.

The path of seeking to understand instead of to be understood was revealed to me during treatment for drug addiction. Bidding adieu to self-centeredness was the first task assigned to me. I resisted, of course, but eventually I saw the light. The Twelve-Step program of Narcotics Anonymous works for me. My Higher Power knows where I went wrong, forgives me, and is busy removing my character defects.

For years, long before I became hooked on painkillers, I avoided seeing myself as I really am. Hitting bottom, acknowledging I was powerless over my addiction, forced me to reevaluate everything I believed in. It was eye-opening.

More than anything, I wanted the peace and serenity the program promised. I was willing to move heaven and earth to get it.

Forgiving the drug-pushing quack who encouraged my addiction was one of the highest hurdles I had to leap, but leap I did. I also made sure he paid for his crimes against humanity (and most especially against Janet Green, Skye Chandler, and myself). Then I had to make amends.

I spent weeks tramping from one house to another in Pine Valley, begging for redemption. To my joyful astonishment, most of the friends and relatives I'd harmed were willing to let bygones be bygones.

One of many hurtful and unfounded labels my detractors love to pin on me is "shallow." They take glee in insinuating I'm less than intellectual. But guess who has the last laugh?

And ALL the way to the bank, too. To everyone who's ever criticised or judged me: I forgive you!

Forgiveness is required even under the most grueling circumstances. Perhaps, as I did, you'll discover buried deep in your psyche terrible things that happened in the past. Don't be afraid to seek professional counseling if you need help. Never fear. As these horrifying memories reveal themselves, take them in hand. You're in charge!

Occasionally sins committed against us are so heinous any thought of charity is driven straight from our minds. These are our greatest challenges.

My father's abandonment, my ex-husband's suit for custody of our daughter, my stepmother and half-sister's treachery, the utter perfidy of my daughter Kendall's unwarranted attacks, Dimitri's betrayal—these are but a few of the battles I've fought. Some were real clashes of Titans, but when the final trumpet sounded the last mournful note— who was the winner? I—who Has It ALL.

If you try your best to show mercy, throw yourself on your knees, humble yourself, ask your Higher Power for help, and the wounds are *still* too raw for forgiveness, I understand. Here's a trick that works for me. When the spirit is willing but the flesh is weak, just plaster a smile on your face and a song in your heart. Whistle, if you want—but not too long. It grates on the nerves.

So what am I advising? Fake it till you make it! That's all. *Pretend* you've extended the olive branch, and before you know it, you have! In no time the halo you earned the hard way will be so shiny it'll glow in the dark. As long as the spirit is willing, you can't fail. Doors you thought had slammed shut forever open effortlessly. Life has new meaning when you turn the other cheek, forgive your enemies.

Above all, don't neglect to forgive yourself. Even if your subconscious blocks out the bulk of your transgressions—as mine did for so long—forgetfulness, like amnesia, is no excuse! You're not exempt from the need for pardon. In fact, you probably need it more.

Seriously! How can you Have It ALL if you harbor resentment against the person you love the most, the person you'll be with until you die, the one you can count on, no matter what? You can't! No self-bashing allowed!

Once you've rooted resentment out of your heart, forgiven everyone who ever transgressed against you, wiped guilt and blame forever off your slate, you're finally ready to exercise your democratic right to life, liberty, and the pursuit of happiness. Go forth and achieve the American Dream!

I've already quoted the clarion call of Greek philosophy: "Forgiveness is better than revenge." They were so right. The Bible, too, hit the nail on the head; but modern philosophers have refined it even further. "Living well is the best revenge," they say.

To that my reply is a hearty "Amen!"

# 9

## *Enjoying It All*

*The National Intruder*, that smutty tabloid poor people buy in supermarkets, once bribed a carpenter to sneak into my house with a camera and take pictures. They ran the photographs with some of the only true words they ever wrote about me, the headline, "Erica Kane Turns Living Well into an Art Form!"

Everything I own is top-drawer. From head to foot, you'll never find me clad in anything but the best. Brilliant designers and plain old garment workers all over the world pay off their mortgages on the money I spend. Even my blue jeans and T-shirts are cut from the finest cotton and hand-stitched.

The same quality is evident in my home furnishings. Each item is carefully selected to reflect my patrician heritage and good taste and is artfully arranged.

I hardly ever hire an interior designer, but when I do, I

(1982; credit: ANN LIMONGELLO/ABC)

I like this shot. Not only do I look great, but it reminds me of my brief fling with Oriental décor.

choose the hottest of the hot. A setter of trends, not a follower. Every few years—or whenever I feel like it—I throw out just about everything in my house and start all over! I can usually accomplish this overnight. Often the transition in furnishings is so smooth, friends and relatives fail to notice.

Wherever I live, I insist on a wine cellar. Even though I don't drink, many of my guests are connoisseurs. I favor French wines from Burgundy or Bordeaux. I also stock port, sherry, and a wide variety of after-dinner liqueurs. Just for the fun of it, I keep my magnums and jeroboams of sparkling spring water in the wine cellar, too.

My jewelry would take your breath away. I have a safe

deposit box full of diamonds, a silver chest overflowing with pearls. I keep my tiaras in a special velvet-lined, burglar-proof cabinet along with my rubies and emeralds.

My real passion is earrings. There's no such thing as too many. I have hundreds!

I wear my jewels! Some might say I flaunt my amazing collection, but why shouldn't I? Kept under lock and key, fine jewels are nothing but a bad investment. You wanted that three-carat pear-shaped diamond set in platinum badly enough to pay for it, or to fight for it in the divorce settlement, so why hide it? Put it on your finger and parade it with pride!

Luxury cars are fast and expensive. I love them. It's delicious to sink into a butter-soft leather bucket seat, grab the steering wheel, and feel the purr of a powerful motor at your command.

I'm an excellent driver. I proved that when I drove one of Travis's Formula One racing cars to victory in the Charleston Grand Prix. I'm also a very safe driver. Unlike most of my friends in Pine Valley, I can count on one hand the number of automobiles I've wrecked.

However, expensive cars do have drawbacks. Carjacking and auto theft spring to mind. Automobile security systems are temperamental, blaring at pedestrians and earthquakes, but rarely at the average car thief who can disarm one in seconds. These alarms are offensive and should be replaced with muscled chauffeurs. Also, when you turn the driving over to someone else, you never have to worry about directions.

Glamorous vacations are a choice Having It ALL perk. Travel is so broadening. You meet such interesting people when you go first class. If forced to choose, I'd probably name Paris as my favorite all-time destination. The city of light! Birthplace of chic! Home of the Mona Lisa!

In my opinion, France is a country that Has It ALL. They only made one big mistake. In the hotheaded fervor of revolution, they guillotined the queen, the ill-fated Marie Antoinette, who Had It ALL but lost her head figuratively, then literally. The lesson there is: Never dismiss crowds of hungry people without bread by saying, "Let them eat cake!"—unless you yourself are supplying the baked goods.

"Adventure travel" is the latest hot rage. I've been doing it for years! When you Have It ALL, don't bother to purchase an adventure travel package. Why pay for it? If you're like me, you'll naturally attract all the adventure you can handle, and then some.

Winter gets old fast. I recommend the Caribbean and South Pacific for international tropical locations. If you're a high-profile celebrity, as I am, you can be sure your privacy will be respected on the gentle islands of these seas.

Beware the tag of "Ugly American." Think of yourself as an ambassador when you travel. Be gracious. Express how charmed you are by quaint local customs even if they repel you. Always get reliable translations of each dish before sampling the cuisine. There are actually countries that relish dining on vermin we leave to exterminators.

If you're introduced to foreign royalty, don't forget:

(1982; credit: ABC)

Crossing police lines to attend a glamorous party.

Americans don't have to curtsy. We're above all that folderol. In our book, everyone's equal, even if some of us are a teensy bit more equal than others.

Foreign travel is superb, especially if you speak the language. Hire a tutor to teach you. A few days of intensive study and you can practically sound like a native. I speak English, a little Latin, and a smattering of French, Spanish, and Italian. A talent for charades is also an asset.

But you don't have to be multilingual or double-jointed to enjoy exotic foreign lands. Everyone speaks English. Yes! Thanks to the sun never setting on the British Empire early in the century and American movies after that, the whole world can understand us! The French hate it, but English is now the language of international commerce.

"See America First" used to be a national slogan, and it should still be. I've been an honored guest of every state of the union. Each is fabulous in its own unique way! From sea to shining sea, there's no place like home.

Hobnobbing with celebrities is tons of fun. As a star myself, I'm not gaga over the thrill, but I won't underestimate the kick of chatting with luminaries like Oprah Winfrey, Betty Ford, Boomer Esiason, Jimmy Buffett, Melba Moore, Donald Trump, Kathie Lee Gifford, etc., etc.!

Having It ALL means feeling perfectly free any time the mood strikes to name-drop. Name-dropping is okay! Celebrities drool to see their names in print. Just make sure you spell them correctly.

I adore being on everyone's A-list. I attend as many parties as possible. I can't accept every invitation, of course, but my calendar is filled with dates for benefit banquets, hoedowns, cotillions, I like them all! I prefer out-of-town parties since Pine Valley galas almost always erupt into mayhem. Oh, well. That's part of the fun.

Yachts, corporate jets, private islands in the Bahamas never become ho-hum. Privileged people at play is and always has been high culture. This is a solemn responsibility. Playing well with others is one more form of art.

I've already shared that one of my hobby/investments is art collecting. My walls are covered with works by the masters. Local artists are my passion. Fans know me as a generous patron of Jeremy Hunter, Stuart Chandler, and Pierce

(1986; credit: ANN LIMONGELLO/ABC; w/STEVIE WONDER)

My good friend Stevie Wonder serenades me.

Riley. I worship Stuart's watercolors, Pierce's sculpture, Jeremy's sensitive portraits, especially if I'm the model.

I certainly don't scrimp on my library, either! Some pointy-headed pseudo-intellectuals think you can tell everything about a person by what's on their bookshelves. What claptrap!

I read voraciously. My bookshelves are stuffed with everything from *Beowulf* to Stephen King. I have six complete sets of encyclopedias and a wing of leather-bound copies of magazines featuring articles about me.

Romantics like me can't get enough poetry. It's in our blood. Poetry speaks to my soul. With a few well-chosen

115

The Metropolitan Museum in New York City was the backdrop for this gig.

words, a poet can make your day. Here's an example I know by heart. Emily Dickinson wrote: "Hope is the thing with feathers—/That perches in the soul—/And sings the tune without the words—/And never stops at all. . . " Isn't that beautiful? Can't you feel it in *your* soul?

Enjoying it ALL includes household help. Hiring a domestic staff to run your home requires specialized skills, aptitude, and finesse. You want helpers you can trust. Workers highly motivated to do things your way. Nannies and governesses with unassailable credentials. With that kind of staff, your home runs like a dream.

How do you find chefs trained in Paris, housekeepers who love to iron, gardeners who treat your roses like their own? The secret is simple, and twofold. First, after you've thoroughly checked out their references, of course, pay them well. Not just the going rate! More! Pay them what *you'd* want to be paid to do the same job; or at least what you'd pay a member of your own family. Second, obey the Golden Rule. Treat household workers with the respect they deserve. That's it. If you'd known it was that easy, you'd have hired a domestic staff long ago—right? I knew it.

Watch out for middle-aged housekeepers. They may seem to be prim and proper, motherly types, but in my experience, they're often demons. If your beloved has a housekeeper who doesn't like you, make him fire her. I guarantee it'll save you big trouble, possibly even your life.

Stable boys are also dangerous. Like cowboys, these restless young men are usually far too independent to work well with others. I don't have to spell out the kinds of difficulties

44

that can bring. I recommend hiring tomboys instead. They're harmless, cheerful, and there's nothing they'd rather do than clean out a stable.

Those of us who Have It ALL are regularly honored by invitations to join things, like clubs, societies, groups whose purpose is either social or philanthropic. These organizations offer big rewards. They have marvelous fund-raising parties. The community service they provide is inspirational.

Just be careful not to spread yourself too thin. My dear friend Phoebe Wallingford beseeches me yearly to join her club. The Daughters of Fine Lineage is a group of women brought together by their dead ancestors. I'd love to be a member, but my crowded schedule prevents it. Pick and choose cautiously where you invest your time and efforts. The rewards, when you reap them, are immense!

When you find yourself perched on the pinnacle of success, you're poised to pick and choose from among the best entertainment out there. Can't you see yourself at the French Open, bullfighting in Spain, at Istanbul's bazaar, mingling with the glitterati at Carnival in Rio? All are yours for the plucking!

You don't have to fly your private jet abroad in order to take advantage of world-class entertainment. You can clap your hands and have it in your own home.

Often the simple pleasures are the most rejuvenating. I sometimes soak in a fragrant bubble bath while I listen to a symphony on my CD player or watch a PBS opera on the television installed above the tub. If I'm feeling nostalgic, I might watch home videos while I sip sparkling cider.

There's no end to the ways you can entertain yourself when you Have It ALL! You're limited only by your imagination, or lack thereof.

If you're lucky enough to be a parent, much of the enjoyment you'll receive from Having It ALL will be showering your children with the advantages of wealth and power. As with everything you do for young people, you'll have to research diligently everyone you hire, every camp or school you send them to, even their Brownie leaders and little playmates. When it comes to our children, we can never be too careful.

I've already covered Bianca's love of horses. She'd rather vacation at a dusty dude ranch than be pampered for a week at an elegant spa. Basking in the light of my daughter's happy smile is the best enjoyment on earth!

I also love to take her shopping. Bianca's wardrobe is almost as extensive as mine. I expect to see her name pop up on best-dressed lists any time.

Having It ALL and enjoying it isn't only about spending money, though. A quiet stroll through the woods or along t' beach with a loved one can create as warm an inner glo' sailing the fjords on a sleek seagoing yacht.

The important thing is to appreciate the lucky sta' which you, like me, were obviously born. Share you' Give unstintingly of yourself. And, above all, c attitude of gratitude.

*Bon voyage, bon appétit, bonne chance!*

# 10

*Erica's Final Ten Tips*

# ONE

Be a good citizen.

If you're an American, Having It ALL is your birthright. America's been good to you. Be good to it in return. This is a sacred obligation. Your country needs you.

It's shocking that only about half of us vote in presidential elections! What's wrong with that other half? Don't they know "we the people" are in charge? If we don't vote, how will our elected officials in Washington know how to be our public servants?

But just voting isn't enough. There's a lot more involved in good citizenship. You have to set a proud example. Fasten your seat belt, wear a helmet when you bike, obey speed limits, remain seated until the captain has brought the aircraft to a complete stop.

Respect every officer of the law you come in contact with, even if he or she is writing a ticket you don't deserve.

When you apply for a driver's license, sign the organ donation card. Why not? Unless it's against your religious principles, what do you care what they do with some parts you no longer need? Waste not, want not. Your spirit's flown yet you still have the power to conquer death! Your heart or your kidney or liver can help someone else live! Think about it! You can Have It ALL—forever!

Give blood. Be bountiful! It takes less than half an hour, doesn't hurt very much, and it's *needed*. Good citizens donate blood at least twice a year, more often if their blood type is rare.

Salute the flag, sing "The Star-Spangled Banner," be patriotic every day, not just on the Fourth of July.

Even if you've been imprisoned for felony crimes you didn't commit, or someone you love has had to withdraw from an election because of scandal, or you were falsely arrested, or, heaven forbid, you've experienced any of the other horrible quirks of fate that have befallen me, you have to rise above it, love your country, be a good citizen!

# TWO

"Practice random acts of kindness, acts of senseless beauty."

This is a profound bumper sticker philosophy I try to follow.

If I'm in an airport, for instance, and spot a person with his leg in a cast, using a cane, carrying a suitcase, I dash over and offer to help with the luggage. Fortunately, there's usually someone with me to do the actual carrying while I sign the cast. It's the thought that counts. I cannot overemphasize this.

When it's time to call the floral designer to change the fresh flower arrangements in every room of my house, I collect the long-lasting blooms from the vases, make a bouquet, drive to the cemetery, and lovingly place them by my mother's headstone. Sometimes I leave flowers on the graves of perfect strangers.

Although I hire professionals, I do have a gift for floral design. If I'm in a restaurant, an office, or even someone's home, and I see how a flower arrangement can be improved—without calling attention to myself, I do it! I don't look for thanks, either.

I have given the coat off my back to the homeless. Driving into New York City, I give money to men who wash my windshields with their skullcaps. I never fail to put money in a Salvation Army kettle during the holidays.

Sometimes a smile is both a random act of kindness *and* an act of senseless beauty. However, if the target of your smile isn't known to you, be sure to do it from the safety of your limo.

Be alert to opportunity! Never pass up a chance to be kind for no reason.

# THREE

Never lend money.

Shakespeare said, "Neither a borrower, nor a lender be." And who was it that Jesus threw out of the temple in

Jerusalem? The moneylenders! Usury is a bad, bad practice.

If someone asks to borrow money, tell them to go to a bank. That's what these institutions are for. If you lend money to a friend, you deprive him or her of doing business at a bank, and thus establishing credit. Don't be selfish! A person who Has It ALL isn't interested in putting banks out of business.

If a person you love needs money, and can't get it at a bank for whatever reason, and you're tempted to lend it— don't! If you do, you'll be sorry! This is often called "code-pendent behavior" and is to be avoided at all cost.

If your inner voice tells you to help the person, then open your purse, but don't lend it! Make it a gift! And remember: Gifts have no strings.

If fate magically returned the cash I loaned to friends before I got smart, I could buy meals for hundreds of starving children in orphanages around the world. It hurts to learn things the hard way. That's why I'm writing this book: so you don't have to make the mistakes I did!

# FOUR

Be kind to creatures.

All life is sacred. We share the earth with snakes, yellow jackets, spiders, and weasels for a reason. Don't ask me what the reason is, but I'm sure my Higher Power knows, or those animals wouldn't be here. That's why, even if they're foam-

(1978; credit: STEVE FENN/ABC)

Here I demonstrate my perfect seat.

ing at the mouth, baring their fangs, trying to sink their claws into my jugular vein, I have to respect them.

Never kill an animal unless you're planning to eat it, or it's planning to eat you. Mosquitoes, black flies, ants, gnats, and no-see-ums who think they can feast on my blood soon meet their maker. But if they leave me alone, I grant them the same courtesy. Doing unto others as you would have them do unto you applies to animals as well as people, in my opinion.

Some animals are more sensitive and highly developed than many humans. Bianca swears she has meaningful relationships with horses. My young friend Tim Dillon's mutt, Harold, is a local hero. Some people dote on gerbils, parrots, even cats. Palmer and his first wife, Daisy, had a cat named Bonkers they treated like a king.

If you have a pet, be sure it's neutered. There are too many unwanted kittens and puppies already. Don't add to the casualty list.

I have no pets. Not because I don't love animals, I do! I have a slight allergy to dander that makes it impossible for me to be around furry things for more than a few hours.

Perhaps you're thinking: Erica certainly does wear a lot of fur coats for someone allergic to dander! You'll be happy to know that, thanks to Daisy Cortlandt's ceaseless ranting about animal rights, I've worn nothing but fake fur since the 1980s. Besides, I wouldn't dare wear the real thing in public. Some activist might throw a bucket of red paint on me.

I've had more than my share of nasty run-ins with wild animals. Off the top of my head, I've been bitten by snakes, mauled by a bear, cornered by Dobermans, and thrown from horses. Once I almost fell off an elephant.

When you love yourself, it's easy to forgive even a snake.

# FIVE

Be open to out-of-body experiences.

I'm not joking. I've been in comas, had enough near-death experiences to know there's spooky stuff out there. We're talking about dreams that go on for days and seem so *real*. My friends Tad Martin and Trevor Dillon have endured similarly weird episodes.

Perhaps now you're thinking: Well, Erica did spend time in Oak Haven, the mental hospital near Pine Valley. . . . Good point. Maybe my mystical experiences are the result of some mental synapse gone awry, but I don't think so. I suspect there are forces in the universe beyond our mortal comprehension.

For instance, my mother died in 1994, but that hasn't stopped us from talking. We chat on a regular basis. I tell her my problems, and she says the things she always said, like, "Oh, Erica," and "Are you sure that's wise?" and "I love you." It's exactly as if she's there, I feel her presence, even though I can't see her. How do you explain *that*? There are mysteries out there still to explore, that's how.

You don't have to believe in ghosts or aliens or anything, just be open to the possibility of a positive paranormal influence in your life!

## SIX

Always use good manners.

If you weren't lucky enough to be born into a home where manners were taught and strictly enforced, as I was, you can study and learn from people who were. Or you can read an etiquette book. Unfortunately, most etiquette books are hopelessly behind the times.

My grandmother was an old-fashioned woman with impeccable deportment. She believed a lady's name should appear in the newspaper only three times: when she's born, when she marries, and when she dies.

See how times have changed?

Some general rules of today are: Treat your elders with extra respect, write thank-you notes, chew with your mouth closed, don't park in spaces reserved for the handicapped, be polite even in the face of rudeness, and try to keep your head, even when all about you are losing theirs.

At a formal meal, you mustn't start eating until everyone is served and the hostess has picked up her fork. Don't forget to tuck your napkin into your lap.

After you've mastered the rudiments of civilized behavior, it's okay to improvise. Since manners vary from country to country, you can term yourself "international." When you Have It ALL, people will accept just about anything.

## SEVEN

Indulge your inner child.

Play! It isn't just for children. Adults need it, too! We all recall fondly the innocent pastimes of our childhood. I can close my eyes and vividly resurrect my eight-year-old self, dazzled by fireflies, playing hide-and-seek in the summer dusk. Those were the days.

If you don't have children of your own to play with, borrow some. Play hopscotch with your niece or your gardener's daughter. Practice alone first so you'll have at least a chance to beat them.

Jump rope. Not only is it one of the most efficient workouts available, it also brings back cherished schoolyard memories. Tag, Red Rover, and Dodge Ball are wholesome, healthy games you can play with just about anyone.

If you feel you didn't have enough toys as a child, buy yourself some! I always wanted an elaborate dollhouse when I was a little girl. My mother said we couldn't afford it. Finally, after I'd worked as a model for several years, I saw the perfect dollhouse in an antique store window, and bought it!

How I loved that toy. I furnished it with tiny, hand-crafted furniture and populated it with ceramic dolls. Unfortunately, when Bianca was quite young, she burned it down.

Wear baby doll pajamas, or—if you're a man—flannel PJ's stamped with trains or cowboys.

Eat comfort food. A bowl of steaming hot oatmeal sprinkled with cinnamon candy hearts instantly re-creates the kitchen I knew and loved as a child. So does a cup of hot cocoa. When my inner child needs pampering, I crave rice pudding, egg custard, macaroni and cheese. Fattening, I know, but naturally I don't overindulge.

On my way to the winner's circle!

The most petite person on the team can score if they know the right moves.

## EIGHT

Wear a watch.

I realize this sounds like a strange tip for Having It ALL, but trust me. A watch can be your best friend.

Nobody can be successful without discipline. Punctuality is an important element of discipline. How can you be on time if you don't wear a watch?

A watch doesn't have to be a tacky ten-dollar piece of plastic junk, although cheap ones have their place and keep time perfectly well. A watch can and should be a major piece of jewelry.

A beautiful watch is a gentle reminder of the old axiom, "Time is money." It's true. People who love themselves and Have It ALL are punctual.

Our grandparents worked a lifetime to earn a gold watch at retirement. Why wait? Run out and buy yourself a state-of-the-art, battery-operated, waterproof, diamond-encrusted gold watch right now!

## NINE

Be prepared.

The simple Boy Scout motto says it all. Set goals, do your homework, get ready for whatever fate throws at you, and you'll always come out the winner! How can you fail? Everyone loves a Boy Scout.

Life is a journey. You don't start a trip without knowing where you're going. You need a map. Several maps, maybe, because there's no such thing as being too prepared. The more you learn ahead of time, the less you have to figure out on the spot. This reduces stress as well as ensuring more time. Always remember that getting there is half the fun.

Whatever you fear is what you must do. If you're afraid of heights, be prepared! Make a plan, do research—then climb that mountain!

You can't, of course, prepare for everything. Curveballs are part of the game. They come flying over the plate just when you least expect them! Don't panic. One wild swing and you're out. Remain calm. No one can destroy your winning streak unless you let them!

# TEN

Don't resist change.

Change is opportunity. People who Have It ALL are exhilarated by change! We thrive on challenge. Even if it's a change we don't like, we adjust! Cheerfully.

They say the only constant is change, and they're right. Learn to welcome it.

Progress can't happen without change. So even if it looks scary, you have to embrace it. Technology is a good example. My brother-in-law Edmund Grey, also a writer, and coauthor of *Erica Kane: Beyond the Pain*, resisted electric typewriters first, then compounded the error by balking at computers. Poor Edmund had to learn the hard way that computer-based technology is here to stay.

Sociologists claim the older we get, the more we resist

One of the most all-time glorious photos ever snapped.

change. Television buys into this theory. Most programmers ruthlessly discount everyone in the audience older than forty-nine. Oldsters are too set in their ways, they say, unlikely to purchase the advertisers' products. As my friend Trevor would say, "What's wrong with this picture?"

People who Have It ALL greet progress with glee no matter how old we are!

# 11

## Q & A

$\mathcal{I}$ get letters. As I noted in the beginning, bagfuls pour into my office every year from loyal fans. Of course I can't read them all! But my industrious staff lives to read my mail; they tell me what people want to know.

I've already explained the big picture. Now I'll answer a few of the more challenging questions.

♥ ♥ ♥ ♥ ♥ ♥ ♥ ♥ ♥ ♥ ♥ ♥ ♥ ♥ ♥ ♥ ♥ ♥ ♥ ♥ ♥ ♥ ♥ ♥ ♥ ♥

*Q:* What *haven't* you done?

*A:* Flown in space. I'd love to suit up as an astronaut and blast off on a shuttle mission to the moon. I also haven't given birth to a son or twins yet, come to think of it, and thanks to excellent DNA, I don't have a single gray hair. Alas, no decorations by Congress, jogs to McDonald's with the President, or audiences with Queen Elizabeth II, either. I can't play the piano. I haven't opened on Broadway yet or won the Nobel Prize. Hmmm. This list is depressing me. On to the next question!

♥♥♥♥♥♥♥♥♥♥♥♥♥♥♥♥♥♥♥♥♥♥♥♥♥♥♥♥♥♥♥

*Q:* Of all of your husbands and lovers, who was the best?

*A:* My goodness, what a question! All my husbands were best, in their time. I learned major life lessons with each. Sometimes more than one lesson per man. Starting with Jeff Martin, they taught me different things about love. Without the benefit of gifted teachers, I'd never be as wise as I am now.

*Q.* Who is the love of your life?

*A.* I haven't met him yet.

♥♥♥♥♥♥♥♥♥♥♥♥♥♥♥♥♥♥♥♥♥♥♥♥♥♥♥

*Q.* What was your favorite job?

*A.* I loved them all! Even the most menial work was pure joy. I've been a salesperson, hostess, model, disco owner, actress, editor, spokesperson, talk show host, entrepreneur, captain of the cosmetics industry, and writer so far. In jail, I swabbed floors, worked in the prison laundry, waited tables. As a mother, I chauffeur, teach, nurse, lifeguard, cook, clean, clothe, etc., etc. Motherhood is a job that never ends.

♥♥♥♥♥♥♥♥♥♥♥♥♥♥♥♥♥♥♥♥♥♥♥♥♥♥♥

*Q.* Who is your best friend?

*A.* In alphabetical order: Opal Cortlandt, Nick Davis, Trevor Dillon, Myrtle Fargate, Janet Green, Joe Martin, and Jackson Montgomery.

*Q.* What about your daughter Kendall?

*A.* What about her? Everything there is to be said on that sorry subject has been said to death, frankly. I forgive Kendall for her trespasses against me. She knows the rules. Whenever she's willing to follow them, she's welcome in my life. Until then, she can stay in Florida where she belongs.

♥♥♥♥♥♥♥♥♥♥♥♥♥♥♥♥♥♥♥♥♥♥♥♥♥♥♥♥♥

*Q.* Why do you use so many clichés?

*A.* Because they save time! Time is money. A penny saved is a penny earned, and getting the point across is what counts. We can't all be poets, for heaven's sake. What care I?—I'm Erica Kane!

♥♥♥♥♥♥♥♥♥♥♥♥♥♥♥♥♥♥♥♥♥♥♥♥♥♥♥♥♥

*Q.* You wear earrings every day and your ears are not pierced. How come?

*A.* Ouch! I like my body too much to puncture it. I don't want any holes in my ears or tattoos, thank you! I will admit, however, that it is a royal pain to take off an earring every time the phone rings.

*Q.* When you carry luggage, why does it never seem heavy?

*A.* I pack light.

♥ ♥ ♥ ♥ ♥ ♥ ♥ ♥ ♥ ♥ ♥ ♥ ♥ ♥ ♥ ♥ ♥ ♥ ♥ ♥ ♥ ♥ ♥ ♥ ♥ ♥ ♥ ♥

*Q.* Do you believe in free love?

*A.* Certainly not! I respect myself way too much to give anything for free. Besides, promiscuity leads to disease. Except for three or four minor exceptions, I never sleep with a man unless I'm in love with him.

♥ ♥ ♥ ♥ ♥ ♥ ♥ ♥ ♥ ♥ ♥ ♥ ♥ ♥ ♥ ♥ ♥ ♥ ♥ ♥ ♥ ♥ ♥ ♥ ♥ ♥ ♥ ♥

*Q.* Why do you always wear high heels?

*A.* I'm not tall. Increasing my height by three inches makes me feel more alive, more powerful, more grateful for my many, many blessings. I can afford to wear high heels every day because I take magnificent care of my feet. I have a pedicure every two weeks, walk barefoot on the beach, and—it goes without saying—I buy only the highest quality footwear and make sure it fits. Proper fit is the secret to comfort.

*Q.* How did you manage to look glamorous in prison?

*A.* Admittedly it was a challenge after my uncouth cellmate Belle confiscated my hot rollers and hairdryer. But there's no excuse for poor hygiene. I don't care if you're on Death Row, you owe it to yourself to look fabulous all the time. Prison ensembles are worse than potato sacks. There's not much you can do to improve your looks behind bars, especially since they don't allow belts. A neat, clean appearance is the most you can hope for, along with an early release.

♥ ♥ ♥ ♥ ♥ ♥ ♥ ♥ ♥ ♥ ♥ ♥ ♥ ♥ ♥ ♥ ♥ ♥ ♥ ♥ ♥ ♥ ♥ ♥ ♥ ♥ ♥ ♥

*Q.* What was the most embarrassing thing the press ever reported about you?

*A.* There are far too many to choose. The major drawback of fame is notoriety. It's horrible to walk down the street, with people pointing at you, shaking their heads. I'm embarrassed the public's viewed my dirty laundry, but *c'est la vie.* What can I do? It's spilled milk under the bridge now, but everything negative ever said or written about me hurts my feelings.

*Q.* Why do you never gain weight?

*A.* By the grace of genetics, I'm one of those lucky people who can live on milkshakes and chocolate sundaes with whipped cream and sprinkles and never gain an ounce. It's wonderful to be me!

♥ ♥ ♥ ♥ ♥ ♥ ♥ ♥ ♥ ♥ ♥ ♥ ♥ ♥ ♥ ♥ ♥ ♥ ♥ ♥ ♥ ♥ ♥ ♥ ♥ ♥ ♥ ♥ ♥

*Q.* Do you have regrets?

*A.* Euuuw! I hate that word. Yes, I have regrets, but not many. I wish my father had been a nicer person, had stayed married to my mother, and had loved us forever. I wish I'd been able to love one man, forever, myself. I regret trusting the wrong people. I'm also sorry for the harm I accidentally caused over the years.

♥ ♥ ♥ ♥ ♥ ♥ ♥ ♥ ♥ ♥ ♥ ♥ ♥ ♥ ♥ ♥ ♥ ♥ ♥ ♥ ♥ ♥ ♥ ♥ ♥ ♥ ♥ ♥ ♥

*Q.* What's the wickedest thing you ever did?

*A.* I'm amazed by how often I'm asked this question. The answer is: I have no idea. My life is an open book—three books, actually. Take a look and decide for yourself.

*Q.* If you had to live on a desert island for ten years and could only take three things, what would you choose?

*A.* Oh, dear. First, I'd take a man, of course. Then I'd probably pack one of my encyclopedia sets so we'd have something to do when we weren't chopping coconuts. And finally, I'd take enough gold to bribe my way off the island if it got too boring.

♥♥♥♥♥♥♥♥♥♥♥♥♥♥♥♥♥♥♥♥♥♥♥♥♥♥♥♥♥♥

*Q.* Do you have a formula for a happy life?

*A.* Yes, I do. It was part of the eulogy Jesse Hubbard, now deceased, gave for my friend Opal's daughter Jenny Nelson. Jesse said, according to Jenny, you only need three things in life to be happy. Someone to love. Something to do. And something to believe in. That's my formula. I follow it. It works!